IMPROVE YOUR SOCIAL SKILLS

The Guidebook to Increase Success in Business
& Relationships, Talk To Anyone Using Effective
Public and Practicing Mindfulness Speaking
& Powerful Communication Training

DANIEL CHARISMA, ROY WENDLER BRIGGS

© Copyright 2020 by (Daniel Charisma, Roy Wendler Briggs)

All rights reserved.

This document is geared towards providing exact and reliable information regarding the topic and issue covered. The publication is sold with the idea that the publisher is not required to render accounting, officially permitted, or otherwise qualified services. If advice is necessary, legal or professional, a practiced individual in the profession should be ordered.

From a Declaration of Principles which was accepted and approved equally by a Committee of the American Bar Association and a Committee of Publishers and Associations.

In no way is it legal to reproduce, duplicate, or transmit any part of this document in either electronic means or printed format. Recording of this publication is strictly prohibited, and any storage of this document is not allowed unless with written permission from the publisher. All rights reserved.

The information provided herein is stated to be truthful and consistent, in that any liability, in terms of inattention or otherwise, by any usage or abuse of any policies, processes, or directions contained within is the solitary and utter responsibility of the recipient reader. Under no circumstances will any legal responsibility or blame be held against the publisher for any reparation, damages, or monetary loss due to the information herein, either directly or indirectly.

Respective authors own all copyrights not held by the publisher.

The information herein is offered for informational purposes solely and is universal as so. The presentation of the information is without a contract or any type of guarantee assurance.

The trademarks that are used are without any consent, and the publication of the trademark is without permission or backing by the trademark owner. All trademarks and brands within this book are for clarifying purposes only and are owned by the owners themselves, not affiliated with this document.

TABLE OF CONTENTS

Introduction 1

Section I: The Core Issue 4

Chapter 1: Poor Social Skills - The Initial Roadblock In Real Expansion 5

    Let Us Begin With Some Self - Introspection: 5

  Social Skill Is A Skill. It Isn't A Gift 8

    We All Love To Live In Our Comfort Zones, And Our Mind Knows It 12

Chapter 2: Factors Behind Weak Social Skills 17

    In Born Traits 18
    Reactive By Nature 19
    Introverts 21
    Gifted Personalities 22
    Adamant Personalities Resisting Change 23

  Inclination 24

    The Stand - Alone People 25
    Lack Of Social Education 26
    Picking Poor Role Models For Mimicking Social Skills 27
    Sheltered Childhood 28
    History Of Getting Ridiculed 29
    Physical Difference As The Reason For Being Mocked 30

  Other Reasons To Get Mocked 32
  A Few Other Things That Can Lead To Poor Self - Image 33

    Tragic Childhood Experiences 33

  Threatened Childhood 34
  Abuse 34

 Social Factors 35
 Mental Health Issues 36

Chapter 3: Impact Of Poor Social Skills On Relationships 37

Chapter 4: Impact Of Poor Social Skills On Work And Business 43

 Which Social Skills Do Employers Want? 46
 Communications Skills To Improve Higher Engagement 48

Chapter 5: Main Areas Of Focus In Social Skills 52

 Conversation Skills To Talk To Anyone Without Hesitation 56
 Better Listening Skills To Be Able To Understand 58
 Skills To Build Confidence 60
 Understanding And Carrying Out Non - Verbal Communication 69
 Understanding And Carrying Out Verbal Communication 70
 Assertiveness 72

Section II: Everything Begins By Understanding The Mind 75

Chapter 6: Fear And Anxiety - The Famed Foes 76

 The Spotlight Effect 79

Chapter 7: The Correct Way To Begin - Improving Your Social Skills 83

 Dealing With Lack Of Motivation 85
 Easing The Pressure 92

    Addressing The Inner Inhibitions 96
    Dealing With Bullying And Traumatic Past 103
    Learning To Work With Your Challenges 105

Section III: Improving Conversation Skills 107

Chapter 8: The Correct Way To Begin - Improving Your Social Skills 108

Chapter 9: Adapt To Become The Right Person For Having Meaningful Conversations 114

Chapter 10: Coming Out Of The Silence Zone 123

    What If You Hit A Wall 131

Chapter 11: Beginning Conversations 135

    The Opening 136
    Taking Conversations Forward 139
    Bringing Conversations To An End 142

Chapter 12: Beginning Conversations 143

    The Opening 144
    Taking Conversations Forward 147
    Bringing Conversations To An End 150

Chapter 13: Getting Comfortable In Groups 151

    What Makes Group Discussions So Challenging For An Introvert? 151
    Tips To Get Better Share In Group Conversations 154

Chapter 14: Learning To Listen 157

Chapter 15: Understanding The Unsaid 165

    Non - Verbal Cues For Beginning A Conversation 166

Cues Signaling Interest In The Conversation 169

Section IV: Learning To Speak In Public 173

Chapter 16: Anxieties Are Natural - Learn To Keep Them Under Control 174

Tips To Lower Anxiety And Build Confidence ... 177

Chapter 17: Understand The Audience You Are About To Address 183

Chapter 18: Getting Hold Of The Mind And The Matter 186

Chapter 19: Importance Of Control Of Your Voice 194

Parts Of Your Voice You Can Work On 195
Ways To Improve Your Public Speaking Voice .. 197

Chapter 20: The Ways To Be More Convincing 201

Section V: Opening Up To The World 210

Chapter 21: Internalizing The Change And Becoming Self - Aware 211

What Is Self - Awareness? 212
Tips To Improve Your Self - Awareness 218

Chapter 22: Guided Meditation Practice For Self - Awareness Of Thoughts 225

Chapter 23: Preparing To Face The World With Confidence 241

Section VI: Strengthening Friendships And Relationships 246

Chapter 24: Friendships And You 247

Chapter 25: Making Friends As An Introvert 253

Chapter 26: Secrets For Introverts To Maintain
Healthy Relationships 259
Conclusion 266

INTRODUCTION

Social skills are one of the most important skills that we need in our lives. We keep repeating the phrase that man is a social animal but tend to ignore the basic skill that we need to make our presence felt. It is one of the most taken for granted skill, and people mostly learn to be good conversationalists and orators by chance and not by design. This book on social skills will help you in understanding the importance of social skills and explain the ways that can help you develop your social skills.

Congratulations on purchasing this book, and thank you for doing so.

This book has been prepared keeping the importance of social skills in mind and also the lack of awareness about it. Most people believe that just because they can strike a conversation with others, they have great social skills. Verbal communication is only one part of social skills, and it doesn't hold the top spot on the list. This book will help you understand various aspects of social skills and the significance they hold in making us more skillful in dealing with people around us.

I have divided this book into six important sections. The first section will help you understand the significance of social skills and also the causes why some people have poor social skills while others are more outgoing. It will also explain the significance of social skills in relationships as well as work and business.

The second section would help you in building your basics and explain the ways you can adopt to shun your fears. Fear and anxiety are your biggest enemies when it comes to social skills, as people are more concerned about the opinion of others about them even more than themselves. This section will also help you understand the basics of skills, such as persuasion and negotiations.

The third section would help you in coming out of the silence zone. It will give you important tips on improving your conversations and taking conversations to a fruitful ending.

The fourth section would deal with public speaking and overcoming the fear that's associated with public speaking.

The fifth section will focus on the deeper concepts of social skills that focus on your personal development.

The sixth section has been devoted to honing your social skills for ensuring better relationships as that is a pillar of our lives.

This book has been written in a straightforward and easy to understand way so that everyone can take advantage of this information.

I hope that you are able to take full advantage of this book.

There are plenty of books on this subject on the market; thanks again for choosing this one! Every effort has been made to ensure it is full of as much useful information as possible; please enjoy it!

SECTION I
THE CORE ISSUE

CHAPTER 1: POOR SOCIAL SKILLS - THE INITIAL ROADBLOCK IN REAL EXPANSION

Let us begin with some self - introspection:

Have you always felt shy about speaking to others?

Most shy people do not like to admit this as a fact, but they always try to avoid direct communication with others, and in place of that, they try to communicate through someone they know or someone they can trust.

Has it occurred to you that you might not be comfortable speaking at specific places, like giving a presentation, explaining something to a group, or negotiating something with another team?

It is nothing new. Even confident people can have stage fright or fear to fail, or the fear of embarrassment. However, that's just a momentary fright, and usually, people overcome that fear soon. But, have these fears got stuck with you?

Do you always remain anxious or uncomfortable about such things and try to push them to others or avoid them completely?

Do you tend to feel socially awkward?

Do you lack the flair others unabashedly display on social occasions?

You may pretend to loath that unapologetic display of charm, magnetism, and charisma, but you cannot stop longing to have that kind of confidence. It has magic hidden in it. People seem to feel attracted to such individuals in droves. They become the life of the party while you choose to remain in your comfort zone, nursing your hurt ego.

Do you feel that you have missed the chance to gain social practice and experience?

Do you believe that there is an age up till which you can behave any which way and no one would mind?

Do you really think that you could have done better then and you've missed the bus now?

Now you are hopelessly tied to your self - imposed image, and doing anything would mean acting like a clown?

Growing up, many people believe that they are not as fortunate, as capable, or as unabashed as others who are performing better than them. They leave these shortcomings unaddressed without realizing that the qualities that they are considering natural talents are skills that need to be polished, refined, and established. We are not born with them. We can only be born without the ability to have these skills ever, i.e., deaf, dumb, blind, and fortunately, that's not the case with most of us.

Being born deaf and dumb can be a handicap for many. However, there are examples where people have done things that others believed an impossible feat for a person with such shortcomings. Helen Keller is a brilliant example of this. Although she wasn't born deaf and blind, she contracted scarlet fever at the age of 19 months and had to live the rest of her life as dead and blind. Yet, it couldn't stop her from learning and performing music. People with no hands have learned to paint with their feet and mouth. People with no legs have performed in gymnastics. There are countless examples to prove that any shortcoming is entirely perceptual.

Social Skill Is a Skill. It isn't a Gift

Social skill might look like a natural talent as we do not study them in our classes. What most people fail to recognize early on in their lives is that social skills need to be acquired. You need to learn them anyway. Some people have a natural acumen for public speaking, and they have lower inhibitions than others. Although that gives them an edge, it doesn't stop you from acquiring these skills.

You can have a different learning pace for social skills, but that doesn't mean you can't learn it as well as others do. It isn't something that you possess. On the contrary, it is a skill that you acquire.

The very outspoken kids in the class either have a very supportive environment at their hand or a group where they are learning to speak or watching others talk well and get recognition, and hence they become outspoken by inspiration. It is the primary stage of learning to speak. Leaving your inhibitions aside is relatively easy at this stage. However, it is a misconception that you can't do that at any other stage of life.

The first thing to understand is that social skills are not inborn.

Some people may have a fair to learn more due to lower inhibitions, but that also comes a lot from the environments they come from initially.

The biggest challenge with social skills is that we never take it as a skill. You believe it to be an inherent quality. Hence, you pay no attention to improve it until a very late stage in life when you are already struggling with communication issues miserably.

If we are performing in any other area in life, like swimming, driving, computer skills, we try to learn and improve. We acknowledge and admit the fact that we don't have those skills or don't possess proficiency in those skills and then practice them. We read about them, train under someone, watch tutorials, and one day we are doing better than others.

When it comes to social skills, we are a fish. No fish needs to teach the baby fish to swim. We believe we still get some coaching in it. Hence, we close our eyes to the fact that we can improve even more in the skill we think we possess since birth.

This mindset makes social skills very difficult to refine.

Our mind is unique and intriguing. At times, it will be very difficult to assess whether you are controlling your mind, or it is controlling you. However, whatever the situation is, the mind always wants the best for you. The problem is that most of the time, its definition of 'the best' is flawed.

Let's see:

Most of us put alarms. To get up on time in the morning. But do you really wake up? There are around 20% of people who wouldn't even budge by the alarm and let us not discuss them here. At best, 10% of people might really get up to the alarm, but 70% of people simply snooze it. Why did they snooze it? They had set the alarm consciously. They wanted to get up.

Let us see what transpired.

There was an impulse that made them snooze the alarm and break the mini - goal. The brain triggered this impulse.

You wanted to lie down or sleep for some more time. The alarm was definitely pushing you to get up, but you wanted some more rest. Your mind understands your needs. It is concerned about your needs.

10% of people got up because they trained their minds to honor the alarm. They conveyed the message that they didn't want the comfort of the best. Sleep was not a problem for them.

Your mind will always keep drawing you towards easy solutions. Snoozing the alarm and going to sleep is easy. The brain wants it. It will help you maintain the same state.

It is Newton's first law of motion called 'inertia.' A body tends to remain in the same state until and unless an external force is applied to it. If you train your mind to work hard, it will push you to do so. You train it to go easy on things, and it will make you do the same.

If you choose the way of comfort and security, your brain will keep drawing you towards the black hole of mediocrity. It will keep doing the things you want. It will drag you into your comfort zone. It will never let you venture out and explore.

If you feel that socializing with others or speaking in front of others may lead to embarrassment, your mind will make you believe that.

Every negative thought you have in mind works as a trigger to increase the grip of this inertia.

If you are not ready to take a challenge, your mind will devise 100 excuses to procrastinate.

Whatever is running at the back of your mind, all your fears, worries, and inhibitions, your mind is reading them. You can't fool it.

If you really want to do something, you'll have to think that way. You will have to think positive. Negative or unwilling thoughts will propel you towards not doing it.

Before you convince anyone else of anything, you will have to convince yourself.

It is a primary problem.

Anything that you do not like, your brain will make you run away from it. Shirk away from doing it. You will have to take charge of your brain.

We all Love to Live in Our Comfort Zones, and Our Mind knows it

No one likes pain or uncomfortable situations. Yet, most achievements require enduring pain and facing hardships. The biggest reason people fail is that their brain convinces them otherwise.

It will try to make you believe in either of the two things:

1. It can devise a better, easier, and painless way to do it later on
2. The end result is not worth the pain and suffering, and other things have better prospects

If your brain becomes successful in convincing either of these things to you, then it is 'game over' for you.

If you want to achieve anything, overcome your fears, or become successful, then you will have to beat this thinking. Life can be as hard as it gets sometimes, and you will have to face it bravely. Facing situations gives you first - hand exposure. You get the unique opportunity to deal with it. Shying away from it will keep pushing you in the corner while the problem keeps getting bolder.

All your fears and inhibitions are the sum total of your thoughts and visualization

Good, bad, ugly or beautiful, lovely, and frightening all these abstract feelings and emotions are a product of our thoughts. Your mind perceives them in your instructions and reactions. Your reactions are inspired by the actions or words of others.

They are nothing more than that. If you are determined, there is nothing to fear. Your brain does not know fear. It does not fear anything.

The fear you feel is out of the accumulated experiences and your perceptions. You will have to overcome your fears by facing and understanding them. Without this, you can never change your mind or learn social skills.

Fear of failure is one of the biggest fears. We are afraid of the social consequences of failure more than the failure itself.

- What would others say?
- How would your neighbors react?
- How would you face your friends?
- What will be the reaction of the crowd?

These are strong fears. But, if you analyse them closely, you'll find that they have little impact on your life in total. A small fear enters your mind and then keeps building its territory over time. By the time you have to face the same situation again, it gets so strong that it overpowers you. Do not let hypothetical situations gain control of your actions. Learn to live life without fear.

The brain has a very sophisticated mechanism. It works with the sole aim to keep you safe and away from harm's way. To this end, it has learned that doing familiar things and not doing many things is safe.

- If there is something that needs extra effort, you would want to procrastinate.
- If there is any amount of risk of failure in some work, your mind would want to abort it
- If you are at the receiving end of a punishment for a mistake, your mind will generate a flight response
- It doesn't want to test its boundaries until you force it to do so. Once you make it do that, the possibilities are limitless.

Social Skill development is a goal that cannot be achieved without the active participation of your mind. Your mind is a companion; you don't want to act as a deadweight or a liability. You will have to train and convince your brain of your intentions. You will have to make your determination clear and affirmative. You will have to make your brain your ally, and then only you will be able to achieve your goals of success.

Coming out of the comfort zone and doing what your brain is not accustomed to is the hardest part. It will test you. Tempt you and even put obstacles like fatigue and distractions. If you can change your mind, you will be able to master your life and achieve success.

Now we will learn the step - by - step way to train the mind.

CHAPTER 2: FACTORS BEHIND WEAK SOCIAL SKILLS

These issues may generally lead to a lack of confidence, self - worth, and uneasiness to interact with others. They might not be the exact cause of poor social skills, but they are behind them. An understanding of these can help you identify the problem, and you can begin working on the solution from there.

- Insecurity and lack of self - worth about themselves
- Doubt about their ability to perform in public spaces
- Anxieties and worries in social situations
- Inability to gain social practice and experience
- Incorrect upbringing or living with people having unsocial behavior

We can put these factors under these specific categories:

In Born Traits

We are all born with some personality traits that give us our character. But that doesn't mean they can't be changed or they can make us poor at social skills. However, it is a fact that some people find it very easy to mix with other people and understand what others want to say. Patience, empathy, tolerance are some of the qualities that some people possess more than others. It gives them the advantage of being more social.

Even if you do not possess them, there is no reason for you to worry because all these traits can be learned and inculcated. The purpose of bringing them up here is to simply explain the reasons you might find it hard to mix well with others or feel awkward at things that others can do effortlessly.

You can develop social skills irrespective of the inborn traits you may possess or the kind of atmosphere and exposure you got while growing up. These things will only help you understand the cause of difficulties you might face in interacting with others as openly some of your peers.

Reactive by Nature

Every individual has the ability to take risks. Still, some people are more risk - averse than others. They tend to react more aggressively. Most people with poor social skills fall into this category. They do not want to take the risk of approaching others and then face rejection. They choose to stay away from the people who can reject them.

These people fear being criticized by others or made fun of, and they want to avoid situations that may lead to such embarrassments. Stage fright or the fear of public speaking is one such fear that seeps into people because they fear that they might not be able to perform, and people would make fun of them. They have very thin skin.

Does that mean such people won't be able to speak on stage or will never be able to do public speaking?

It will be a premature conclusion. The people who have a fear of public speaking are not short of words or knowledge, but they haven't received the right kind of exposure and training. They can speak as eloquently as others, not having stage fright if they begin with a smaller audience with familiar faces and then go on to a larger audience. Practice and exposure can help them overcome the stage fright easily. But, people with poor social skills generally take it as their fate to never give it a thorough try.

These people can get stimulated easily, and even a small hint of discouragement or disapproval, in the beginning, can make them give up forever. It is the reason it remains such a big challenge for most people.

The important thing to understand here is that we all have insecurities and weak points. Having a fear of failing is nothing to be ashamed of. However, not even trying to overcome that fear is can be a lifelong impediment that you will need to overcome.

If you have a highly reactive nature, you will have to begin trying with a smaller group of people you trust. Once you feel confident enough, you can begin speaking on things you know with great clarity. Soon you'll find that there is nothing that can stop you from speaking even in large groups or even in front of a large audience.

Introverts

Being introvert is a choice and not a compulsion imposed on you. Most people like to believe that they are introverts by nature, and there is no way they can be more open. It is a misconception. Choosing to stick with yourself is always a choice. You wear loneliness and seclusion as a protective shield around you.

It is a fact that while some people may love calm and peace more than others, it wouldn't make them uncomfortable when they are in a crowded place. Their soul only yearns for calm to think better and feel at peace.

However, if you are an introvert by choice, you'll feel uncomfortable at places where you have to talk to others or actively participate in anything. It is a sign of poor social skills.

Most people don't like to go clubs not because they despise the sound in the clubs but because they can't dance well, and they fear they might look awkward. Such people never peek inside and see that most of the people on the dance floor don't know how to dance either. They have low inhibition levels, and they simply don't care what others think about their dance as they have gone there to enjoy themselves.

There is nothing wrong with being an introvert by nature. You get more time for yourself, and you will be in a better position to work on other aspects of your personality and accumulation of knowledge. However, it shouldn't be used as an excuse simply because you do not want to learn to interact with others.

Gifted Personalities

These are the people who really believe that they are in a disadvantageous position for developing social skills. For developing great social skills, you need to have a circle. However, gifted individuals who are more intelligent and creative may not find people with whom they can relate. Such individuals may find it hard to bring themselves to the level of others around them, and they choose not to mix.

However, by doing so, they'll be doing a great disservice to themselves. Irrespective of the intellectual genius such individuals may possess, they'll ultimately need to serve their gift to these very people, and then they'll fail miserably.

Sometimes intellectual genius fills people with pride, and they don't feel like interacting with ordinary people, and they begin to think everyone beneath them. It is again going to harm them in the future. Ultimately when they have to interact with people at later stages, they might find it very hard to adjust.

It is a myth created by some people that gifted individuals with high IQ will always remain as social misfits. There can be a certain degree of uneasiness, and they may prefer more to keep to themselves, but there is nothing that stops them from developing good social skills. In fact, if they try, they can develop better social skills due to their high intelligence level and find it easy to navigate.

Adamant Personalities Resisting Change

Some people are rigid by nature and the kind of upbringing they have; they resist change. They become adamant. It is not something that they are born with but what they ingrained with.

For instance, if you look at the people who have served in the army for very long, they get used to the routine so much that they begin to loath everything that doesn't follow a routine, and this even includes the things that don't have a routine.

Such people are slaves to predictability and don't know improvisation in real - life situations.

What such people fail to realize is that social skill is a life skill that's not optional. You live in a society, and you can't prevent interactions with other people. If you do not develop social skills, you'll often find yourself at loggerheads with others.

Inclination

People with peculiar interests may also find themselves unable to fit in. It happens because many times, people around them fail to understand them or make fun of them. To prevent themselves from constant interactions and troubles, some people choose to stick to themselves and never develop social skills.

Although it all begins with a problem, not trying to develop social skills or not attempting to find a group where they could fit in would always deprive them of social skills they would need.

There is nothing wrong with having an interest in something different or following your passion, but thinking that you can pleasantly survive on your own is a misconception. The only problem with it is that when you ultimately think of re - joining the society of mixing with others, you'll face great difficulty as you wouldn't remain malleable.

The Stand - Alone People

Some people are different. They might not like to identify themselves in a particular gender bracket or may not appear as others of their type look. It is not a very hard thing to find. You can always find boys that are more on the feminine side, have facial features that may not give them a very masculine appearance. Even some of their habits and behavioural patterns may be on the feminine side. It can happen due to several reasons. But, society likes to brand such people and then pick on them. The same can also happen in the case of girls who start behaving like boys or take tomboy appearance. Even such girls are laughed at by their peers. Such people generally choose to become reserved to prevent the agony of being picked on regularly.

However, the only problem in doing that is they stop trying to learn social skills. As the world brands them in a specific category, even they brand the rest of the world in a specific category and begin to loath it. Such people may have poor social skills as their exposure is low and never really great.

Lack of Social Education

As I mentioned in the beginning that even social skill is a skill as the name suggests. However, people make a half - hearted effort, if any at all, in learning it. Kids usually learn it organically by watching others behave in society. Earlier, it wasn't that difficult when people lived very laid back lives, and everyone knew everyone in the town. It presented ample opportunities for the kids to watch others and learn. It has become a bit difficult in the current times as people have moved to metropolitan cities where that kind of social connect is missing altogether.

Normally, kids still learn it in school and their day to day interactions and through movies, yet it is not the same as getting hands of experience of practicing it themselves. The kids who are socially awkward or don't fit in usually keep away from the crowds and do not get to learn anything properly. Such kids can easily miss social skills.

Picking Poor Role Models for Mimicking Social Skills

We all have grown watching cartoon characters and having some favorites. While captain Popeye gulped cans and cans of spinach, it became relatively easier for mothers to feed vegetables to the kids as they wanted to follow their favorite cartoon.

As we grow, our role models change; however, our trait of picking habits from our favorite characters doesn't change. We all have some characteristics that we can identify with some characters on the TV and Movies. Once we fully identify that character, we attempt to live the life of that character. It makes us feel better and can also make some people feel important. Mostly such characters are central to the story and have some gravitas. We begin to expect the same happening with us, and then the isolation begins.

Some characters of genius people are already represented as misfits, and people have formed a misconception that geniuses are essentially misfits.

Breaking of this myth in your mind is very important. Until you keep thinking about that character as your inspiration, you'll never be able to learn and behave differently. Social skills don't come if you keep sitting under a rock.

Sheltered Childhood

It is again a big cause of poor social skills, and it is increasing at a rapid pace. People these days live a very insecure life. They are fearful of everyone around them, and to some extent, that fear is not unreasonable. They want to keep their kids protected, and therefore, the social exposure of kids reduces significantly.

Kids live a very protected life, and they don't do anything freely, and the pressure on them is so high that they don't get to do much socially. For them, social interaction remains restricted to their parents and siblings and a few hours of exposure at school.

If for some unfortunate reason, their social interaction isn't much at the school, they will not have much social exposure at all. When such kids have to face the society in the open on their own, they might succumb to the pressure and get back inside the cocoon of being an introvert.

Such people aren't introverts; they simply do not possess the social skill needed to help them cope up with the world they have got exposed to right now.

Overprotective parents who try to make their kids a clone of themselves can also become a cause of poor social skills in their kids. They limit the social exposure of their kids and keep a strict watch on what their kids learn. It can make the kids miss out on learning about social skills from the outside world.

History of Getting Ridiculed

As we have discussed, bullying and mocking can be among the primary reasons why many people are never able to acquire social skills. Turning inwards is a desperate attempt made by them to shield themselves from the constant bullying and ridicule that they might be facing.

Some kids and even adults are highly sensitive to the amount fo brick - bat they can take, and when it gets over their limits, they choose to develop tendencies that are not very social. Some of them might even pick violence and revenge as their favorite tool.

The problem with bullying is that one can get bullied even at home, and in that case, there is no place to take refuge. Kids can get bullied or might witness preferential treatment at home that may make them feel socially incapable. Such bullying can come from parents, elders like uncles, aunts, grandparents, and elder siblings. In most cases, the child doesn't even have anyone to reach out, and that feeling of helplessness can push the child towards complete exclusion.

Physical Difference as the Reason for Being Mocked

It world can make fun of anything different. Clowns and dwarfs have remained the medium of entertainment in the circus for longer than we'd like to believe. In the current age, fat - shaming is culturally not acceptable, but who can stop comedians from making a joke on themselves and their obesity. Some people covertly and overtly use fat - shaming as a tool to humiliate others. From long teeth to big nose, everything that's not like others can be made fun of by others.

Some commonly used topics for making fun are:

- Having poor skin
- Having buck teeth, big ears, or anything else like that
- Having a physical deformity or disability
- Racial or ethnic difference

These are just a few things that can be used to mock a kid, and that may make the child feel socially odd or like a misfit. Such mocking can break the confidence of the child or even an adult, and the child may begin feeling secure all alone.

Such mocking has a profound impact on the impressionable mind of the child. There is nothing that child could have done to prevent it, but the next step can surely take the child toward self - exclusion.

The biggest problem with such things is the inability of the child to change anything about it and the helplessness that arises from it. This sense of helplessness and lack of confidence are the biggest hindrances that individuals might face in gaining social skills.

Other Reasons to Get Mocked

Bullying is a crime, but it is a commonly committed crime. Kids may get bullied for several things beyond their control, and they may not have anything in their power to prevent or reverse that.

Some common reasons for getting bullied are:

- Their religion
- Their ethnic background
- Their sexual orientation
- Being poor
- Their unpopular interests
- Family reputation
- Unique first or last name
- Their accent
- Within the family, kids can get mocked or insulted for:

From parents:

- For performing poorly that their siblings
- For being shy

- For not following the right things, they might prefer

In the class, kids can be mocked for:

- Being a shy kid in the class who remains silent most of the time
- For being meek and not speaking up enough
- For being too weak or too fat or too clumsy

A Few Other Things That Can Lead To Poor Self - Image

The worst thing about bullying is that the kid starts becoming underconfident and develops a poor image of the self. This image is very hard to break because it gets cemented in the mind of the child over the years. A poor self - image also comes in the way of learning something new.

Tragic Childhood Experiences

Sometimes kids can lose someone very special in their lives who has been their pillar of support, and they begin crouching inside their protective shell as they fear that anyone else wouldn't be able to provide that kind of love, affection, and support. They never give it a try to look for themselves if the world is fine or not.

Threatened Childhood

People with a turbulent childhood with too much violence and a constant struggle for survival can also turn inwards for survival. They do not find the refuge they have been looking for, and hence they turn inwards.

Abuse

Physical, mental, sexual, and emotional abuse of a child in any manner can make a child feel insecure and turn that person into a loner. Such abuses are highly damaging, and they have a deep impression on the mind of the child. Such kids stop relying on and believing others completely and also have trust issues.

They can become shy and loners. They may be very hard to teach social skills as more than social skills they lack trust. They fear adopting this world in particular.

Social factors

Society is changing rapidly, and it is evident. Any change brings a lot of things with itself. The current society is aggressively fending for itself, and there is a lot of competition, and there are insecurities too. It has contributed largely to the kids being secluded in one corner. The seclusion is not a punishment but the need of the hour too. The influence of cable TV, internet, and social media websites are also very high in this.

The social media explosion is just more than two decades old. The real explosion only came after the Facebook era began, and today there are countless websites of that nature to attract kids.

In this age, it'd be hard to push a kid to play in the ground as the kids are spending more and more time socializing on the internet. Their focus is more on virtual social media networking rather than a real one because they can shut the virtual world anytime they wish.

It is much worse news than it might sound because the kids who have thousands of friends online may not have enough even to count on their fingers, and this gives them a false sense of confidence that can be dangerous when they venture into the real world for work.

Social media is engaging, but it is taking up more time than the kids could afford to give, and in turn, it is giving an experience that may fill them with a false sense of security.

Learning social skills can be difficult even for kids like these when they grow up. The world doesn't work as simple as unfriending a person or blocking them with a click of a button.

Mental Health Issues

Several mental health issues like depression and social anxiety disorders can also make people adopt a lonely lifestyle. Such people are really struggling within their minds and may find coping up with the outside world difficult.

If they do not get the right kind of exposure and support, they might find it very hard to develop proper social skills.

CHAPTER 3: IMPACT OF POOR SOCIAL SKILLS ON RELATIONSHIPS

Social skills are relationship formation go hand in hand. Some relationships are organic—relationship with your parents, siblings, your childhood friends, etc. come in this category. They form without your conscious effort, and it doesn't take much effort to maintain these relationships.

However, relationships at the workplace, at places of education, and stronger personal relationships, later on, are more complex. You have to form such relationships with conscious effort and keep nurturing them all the time. If you stop paying attention to them or become lax in your attitude, such relationships begin to fall apart.

When it comes to personal relationships, most people live in the misconception that they only need love to make a relationship succeed. As I said, this is a misconception. It takes much more than love and understanding. Without two - way communication of any form of your choice, no relationship can survive.

You need social skills for establishing all kinds of relationships, romantic or otherwise. It is not your love and pleasing personality that's going to make people talk to you, admire you, or be friends with you.

From the first interaction that begins with acknowledgment to approaching that individual, friendship, and establishment of a free - flowing communication bridge, it is a process that goes through various stages.

From a child to an adult, everyone must understand that there are eight parts of social skills that you need to master to build relationships. These skills can help you in being more assertive.

Interaction Skills: It is the initial contact you establish with a person. Most people take this part very lightly. Establishing a connection is not all about words. The acknowledging smile, the eye contact, the nodding of the head, all these are signs of your interest in a person. These reflect your interest and your warmth. Most people ignore the importance of this social skill to a large extent. If you walk by a street and cross someone every day, the chances are dim that your face might get etched in the memory of that person. However, if you are the person who smiles every time the eyes meet, that person is more likely to remember you. The same happens in the workplace too. It is your first interaction, and you must always remain liberal while smiling. Always remember a simple rule; anyone who isn't your marked enemy is your probable friend.

Approach Skill: The way to approach a person has been the subject of great research. From finding various one - liners to pick - up lines, people try all sorts of things to approach others. It is a crucial part; your approach must not make someone feel alarmed. If the person you are approaching is afraid or doubtful of your intentions, there might not be any progress at all. It is a part to which everyone must pay great attention.

Engagement with others: There are some common rules and etiquettes that society expects us to know. If you do not know those rules or don't follow them, you can stand out and may face problems in connecting to others. Simple things like sharing with others, waiting, taking turns at things, following the rules, etc. are some of the things that you can't ignore when you are trying to improve your social skills as they make you more genuine and approachable.

Friendship skills: These are the skills people struggle to learn but find hard to master. Friendship is all about inclusion, appreciation, and affection. Most people pay attention to these virtues only half - way, and some don't even show the courtesy of doing even that much, and that can lead to friction. If you want to be someone inclusive and affectionate, you will have to demonstrate the same to others.

Empathy: We all need to have empathy. It is a skill that we all possess but do not exercise properly. Empathy means to feel what the other person is feeling. It isn't an easy task many times. However, relationships can't work without taking into account the perspective of the other person. When you are trying to be more engaging, you will have to stick to relatable things and show that you care. Empathy is a human aspect that we are all born with, but usually, people don't pay much attention to it. For improving your social skills, this is an aspect you must work on.

Communication Skills: As you can see, communication hasn't got first place in social skills. Communication skills are very important for taking any relationship forward and sustaining it, but it doesn't always begin with words. Communication is not about words but the way you are capable of expressing yourself and the opportunity to give others to express themselves. In short, it is about conveying the idea and allowing the flow of information.

Sense of Humor: A good sense of humor is always a very useful trait of social skills as it doesn't let interactions get boring and also helps in diffusing stressful situations. You don't need to be able to crack jokes; simply saying the right things on a lighter note helps.

Ability to Resolve Conflicts: finally, an important part of social skills is to be able to diffuse stressful situations, manage disagreements in an acceptable manner, and negotiate with people.

As you can see, the lack of these skills can have a negative impact on relationships. You may not only face difficulties in forming strong relationship bonds in your personal as well as professional life, but you may also struggle with maintaining those bonds. Therefore working on all these aspects will be a must. We will be discussing these topics in detail ahead in the book.

CHAPTER 4: IMPACT OF POOR SOCIAL SKILLS ON WORK AND BUSINESS

Teamwork, technology, coordination, and communication are some of the most common words you get to hear at the workplace, and indeed they are crucial for your smooth functioning in the work environment.

Lack of communication can be a result of poor social skills, and that may also cause stress, relational breakdown, low morale, and other such chronic workplace issues.

If someone does not have proper social skills, that individual may witness the following:

Workplace Stress: A workplace is not something that runs on an individual. Everyone in the team must remain a part of the communication flow so that things do not get stuck at any point or complacency doesn't set in. However, if a person has poor social skills, it can lead to poor communication that may obstruct the flow of information. Poor social skills may also lead to tense conversations, and there may not be a sense of humor to diffuse the tension. All this can also make it an unhealthy conversation that is counterproductive. All this leads to stress, and the workplace becomes less productive. Good social skills make employees more productive and flexible. They can handle even the stressful situations in a much better way, and that's why preference is given to individuals with good social skills.

Incorrect Expectation Setting: One of the biggest disadvantages of poor social skills is that the individuals are never able to speak for themselves and put their discomfort on the table. It leads to overloading of work or setting up of expectations that can't be met. If social skills are good, you will have the confidence to speak up for yourself artfully so that the load can be reduced and expectations can be kept within manageable limits.

Relational Breakdowns and Arguments: Maintaining cordial relationships at work can be challenging. There is cut - throat competition, and everyone is trying to save their backs. In such conditions, tempers can flare up easily. All this leads to tensions and conflicts arise. The biggest problem lies in reconciliation. You have to work at that place, and hence there will be numerous incidents when you may need to work with the same individual or team. If you keep the conflicts simmering within you, working and making communication flow can be another impediment that you might face. Good social skills help you in reaching a compromise or striking the conversation again.

Health Issues: Poor social skills can increase the stress and anxiety at the workplace, and this may lead to health issues related to your physical and mental health. People are not able to manage their emotions effectively, leading to excessive amounts of stress and anxiety.

Complaints: If social skills are weak, it is easy to falter on communication, and the clients may not take that well. It is one of the biggest reasons people face flak in their workplace. Social skills help you in being open about your position and communicate that to others in a way they can empathize with your situation. If you are blunt about it, the client may not take that well. If you try to hide it, that may again create problems for you.

Healthy social skills help you in navigating the difficulties at your workplace smoothly. You are able to communicate better within the ecosystem of your organization better and also with your clients, bringing a better satisfaction score.

Which Social Skills Do Employers Want?

You can count social skills as the most important soft skills that employers are looking for these days. These are not special abilities that the employers want, but they know that if their employees have social skills, their productivity would certainly increase. Good social skills make the flow of information smooth, and getting work done as a team becomes easier.

There are five social skills that are a must for succeeding at work:

Empathy: As I have always mentioned, empathy is a basic social skill that most employers look for in their employees. It makes working with and understanding others easy. Especially when dealing with the clients, you are able to get to their level and understand what they want. It helps in jobs getting executed faster and better with higher client satisfaction. Higher empathy also helps you in really understanding the problems experienced by your clients, management, and co - workers, and the atmosphere at the workplace can be made more human than robotic.

Teamwork: We do most of the work in teams. But some people are loners. They might be excellent workers, but when it would come to the flow of work, either they'll run faster than the whole team and feel exasperated or work differently than the whole team and bring inconsistencies. Social skills help you in developing an understanding of the value of teamwork and the results it can bring. People with poor social skills always remain stuck at a thorn in the thumb and repeatedly derail the whole work environment.

Communication: Passing on vital information on time is a crucial part of a healthy work environment. Delay in passing information can lead to various lapses. You may have to pass information through verbal and written mediums, and you'll need to be precise and clear in it. That's why it is the favorite social skill employers want to have in their employees.

Non - verbal Communication: What we say and how we say things is important but most of the things are not said in so many words but understood through gestures, eye contact, posture, and facial expressions. Employers like people who have social skills to decipher the meaning and act accordingly.

Listening: We are living in a world full of so much chatter that we have stopped paying attention to the important skill of listening. Most people are ready to jump the gun and reach on wrong conclusions. It is a good thing to pre - empt situations and understand things easily, but if you are a poor listener, employers might not be very happy with you as that can lead to miscommunication. Employers specifically like to hire people who can lend their ears and pay attention to the important detail.

Communications Skills to Improve Higher Engagement

Communication is an important social skill. However, that would be an understatement. In fact, as per James Humes, 'Every time you speak, you are auditioning for leadership.' Your communication power defines your leadership skills. If you are a poor communicator, you will be an ineffective leader. It is not about being an introvert or an extrovert, speaking less or more, it is about conveying the message across the board in the most effective manner, and that must be known to every person in order to perform.

It is your job to engage with people. You must become a people person.

You can't be an ace swimmer if you don't like water. There are no two ways to do it. Whatever be your medium of communication, it must be effective. To succeed, you must have powerful communication skills and uses them even more powerfully.

People usually confuse communication with speech. Speaking is not the only way of communication. We communicate with people on so many different levels. The way we conduct ourselves in the environment, the way to behave, the way we engage, all these things are a form of communication. You must know that people are taking cues for all your actions, and you must always remain conscious of that.

In cross - functional teams where the working steam is very high, there are times when this communication bridge starts breaking. The various communication mediums are also making the communication disconnected and distant, taking away the connection. It deteriorates the engagement with the team and also lowers the effectiveness of the leader.

There are several ways in which you can improve your communication with the team:

Be Concise: It isn't important to speak too much, but it is important that what you say means a lot. You should be concise; it makes the message concrete and helps you in appearing confident. You must speak in certain terms. Ambiguity is neither expected nor desired.

Verify Understanding: People sitting around you would invariably shake their heads in understanding even if they fail to understand you. It is a natural reaction to hide embarrassment or confrontation. However, you must verify it several times to ensure that your message has been conveyed across the board clearly. You can ask your team to repeat the message or their interpretation. It removes the chances of misunderstanding or misinterpretation. It also helps in improving your personal engagement with the team.

Communicate to Make a Difference: Your communication must add something valuable. Speaking something simply for the sake of adding a few more words is never helpful. Everything that you speak must have meaning and should add something valuable to the conversation. Try to exhibit knowledge, power, and expertise, and that should resonate in your communication.

CHAPTER 5: MAIN AREAS OF FOCUS IN SOCIAL SKILLS

Social skill is a very broad subject, and the list of all the social skills can be very long. We'll begin with the primary concept and then explore the advanced skills that may be required for building self - esteem, strengthening relationships, and excelling at your workplace.

Simply put, social skills are the basic skills that you'll need to make your path in the social world. The people living in caves all by themselves didn't need social skills, but when those same people came out of the caves to begin living as tribe people, they also needed social skills.

Most people misunderstand social skills as courtesies and social etiquettes. There is nothing common between both beside the word social. Social skills are purely interpersonal skills that help you in understanding this world better and making sense of it. Think of the world talking in a coded language, and the social skills are that language you need to understand the unsaid things in this world.

Whatever you listen to is direct communication. But does that always mean the same? And I am not talking about homophones.

For instance, let us take the word 'really':

You can use this single word in various tones by raising and lowering your pitch and intonation, and the meaning of the word might change from surprise, doubt, disbelief, to curiosity. You can also use this word to make fun of something said by a person.

People with poor social skills might find it hard to discern the usage of that word in that line.

You will need to understand the meaning, make a judgment of the intention, and take action to prevent escalation in case of negative inference and encourage if it is something beneficial.

Therefore, we can divide primary social skills into three parts:

1. Observing
2. Discerning
3. Committing

Observing

It is the easy part in which you simply observe the action taking place in front of you. It can be a simple hand gesture, raising of shoulders in ignorance, aggressive action, or even playfulness.

Every action doesn't mean the same thing as the word 'really' didn't mean the same. While you read the action of the person in front of you, you also read facial expressions and the tension.

Discerning

In this part, you quickly interpret the meaning of the action you just observed. The decision has to come in a split second, as you may not have very long to think. Here, you can put together all the data like behavior, relationship in the past, any impact of a current event, or any such information in your mind.

Committing

In this step, you need to take action as per the decision. Your action should be in the direction of diffusing a tense situation to the best of your ability and encouraging positive action. Many times, not taking any action is the best action at that moment when you know that no matter what you say, the situation is going to inflame anyway.

These are the three primary social skills that we learn as we grow. All the smart street kids perfect these skills because they are navigating dangerous or stressful situations all the time. However, people who have grown in a protected environment may find it hard to put everything in one place.

As an adult, the primary social skills remain the same; the application and its area can expand endlessly.

The main areas of focus in social skills are:

- Conversation Skills to talk to anyone without hesitation
- Better Listening skills to be able to understand
- Skills to build confidence
- Understanding and carrying out non - verbal communication
- Understanding and carrying out verbal communication
- Assertiveness

Conversation Skills to Talk to Anyone Without Hesitation

It is an important skill for adults as it helps them in having meaningful conversations. Such conversations include telling things, asking questions, responding to others, letting people know your opinion, understanding the opinion of others, keeping people involved, and ending conversations politely on a positive note.

Although most people think that they have the requisite conversation skills, most people may have a hard time holding a meaningful conversation with other people having opposing views.

Within a few minutes of beginning a conversation, most people reach an awkward silence where they can listen to their heartbeats. A large number of people begin serious conversations with an objective but never reach there as they are not able to stick to the subject. Another category is of the people who begin conversations but change it to a duel of words where everyone is speaking, and no one is listening.

As you can imagine, all the conversations would end up being unproductive.

Therefore, the ability to have productive social conversations is a social skill that is on par with others.

We can break conversations into two parts:

- Giving response to something being asked
- Requesting a response regarding the topic in discussion

What most people don't understand is that digressing from the topic is not only unproductive, but it may also drag the conversation into a direction that may not have a positive outcome. You might have observed several people who begin serious conversations and then branch out in the middle. They don't understand that such conversations are not only costing their time but also the time, patience, and energy of the other people who are part of it.

To hold a good conversation, you must have two clear objectives:

- Provide a relevant response to something being asked of you. Your response must not be ambiguous, and it should have a clear meaning in itself.

- When you ask someone a question, you must form the question in a way that the listener knows your intent.

Better Listening skills to be able to understand

Listening skills when you are talking in terms of social skills are not your ability to hear but to listen and understand the meaning. Both have a considerable difference.

It is more like reading between the lines. It is less about words and more about inference. In general, we are in a hurry to spit out a response for whatever is said, but better listening and social skill do not take you in that direction.

Better listening includes giving respect to what the other person has to say. You must exhibit from your behavior that you have a keen interest in that topic, and you are paying attention.

Most people suffer from the problem of talking a lot more than listening. They want to spit out all they have within them and then block their minds to the information coming their way. They are not receptive and highly prejudiced.

Better listening skills means that you listen without any prejudice and try to understand the core of the matter and evaluate the response on merit. If you do not have that skill, you'll soon find that people would also stop paying interest in what you have to say.

Some people begin displaying a fidgety behavior like fiddling with their phones or keep changing positions in their chairs. You must not forget that even the speaker can judge your behavior in the same manner.

Most conversations drift apart from the core issue because you are not asking a clear question. Asking a precise question that elicits the correct and unambiguous question is also an art that is part of your talking skills to carry out a meaningful conversation.

There will be times when the response of the person on the other side may not warrant a response from your side. However, leaving the conversation at that point or ending it bluntly can be awkward, even in that case, physical gestures like nodding in affirmation or saying 'yes' is always helpful.

The last thing in developing better listening skills is to be more receptive to the information you are getting. You cannot allow the information just to cross your ears and pass into oblivion. Remembering what someone has told you is also a part of better listening skills.

Skills to Build Confidence

Confidence makes you look stronger and affirmative. However, the very same confidence that makes you look stronger is very delicate in itself. There is no specific thing that can make you confident. Building confidence is an exercise that includes a lot of things like your posture, your placement of hands, your gait, the way you make eye contact, facial expressions, and, most importantly, your body language.

You might have encountered situations when you went with great confidence and exuberance but came back defeated despite having everything by your side.

How Does That Happen?

The simple answer is intimidation. You get intimidated by the posture and body language of the person in front of you. You don't feel the same amount of confidence in what you are saying, and does it sound the same exhibiting the same amount of confidence you were feeling a few moments later.

If you have watched courtroom drama movies, you might have witnessed that lawyers easily intimidate the people sitting in the questioning box, although they would have been coached by their lawyers thoroughly.

Therefore, it is imperative to understand that overall body language plays an equally important role in making you more convincing.

It would be helpful to understand that as per studies, the contribution of your body language in the communication can be as high as 55%. It is not what we say that matters so much, but how we say that matters.

We'll now touch some important parts of your body language that display confidence.

> **Posture:** Your posture while you talk is very important. When you are talking, you must hold your head straight. Your spine and your head should remain in alignment. While talking, it is always better to keep

your chin bent a little downwards. Hunching on the table or hanging your head while you talk are signs of weakness, fear, insecurities, and shame. Most people do not have control over their posture when they are nervous. It is nothing uncommon. However, you can practice your posture in front of someone you trust and visualize the difference and take mental notes to keep correcting your posture. Also, you need to remember that while you keep your spine erect and your head straight, you must not make your body stiff. Such a posture is difficult to hold for long, and as you begin slouching, you'll lose steam. Therefore, you must keep your body relaxed.

Placement of Hands: Placement of hands is also equally important. Confident people always have their hands visible. Never shove your hands inside your pockets as that would display your discomfort that can alarm other people.

Gait: Walking is an important indicator of the confidence you carry. If you are walking cautiously, taking small steps, or keeping your eyes glued to the floor, it displays your lack of confidence. You must always walk with confidence and long steps keeping your eyes pointed towards your destination.

Eye contact: You must never avoid eye contact. You are talking to that person, and there is no way you can be invisible; therefore, you do not have a cause to avoid eye contact. Avoiding eye contact displays your lack of confidence and anxiety.

Facial Expressions: Facial expressions are the hardest to control because there is a reflex action taking place, and your emotions easily come on your face. However, there are some ways to appear confident at all times. Your smile is your biggest deception. When you have a smile on your face, there is little space left for other emotions. But you must remain cautious with your smile too because smiling too much or even when it isn't needed can be a big give away. You must have a soft and confident smile on your face. Besides smiling, you must not do things like biting your lips, blinking rapidly, or the clenching of jaws as they can show your underconfidence.

Body Language: Body language is very important to reflect confidence. It is very hard to control if you aren't very confident, but some people have poor body language even if they are confident about the things they are saying. Things like keeping your arms crossed while you talk, tilted head, avoidance of eye contact, trying to shift your weight continuously, and tapping of the feet are a few things that can clearly exhibit your anxiety, impatience, and frustration.

You must avoid doing all such things to appear confident in your conversations.

Confidence makes you look stronger and affirmative. However, the very same confidence that makes you look stronger is very delicate in itself. There is no specific thing that can make you confident. Building confidence is an exercise that includes a lot of things like your posture, your placement of hands, your gait, the way you make eye contact, facial expressions, and, most importantly, your body language.

You might have encountered situations when you went with great confidence and exuberance but came back defeated despite having everything by your side.

How Does That Happen?

The simple answer is intimidation. You get intimidated by the posture and body language of the person in front of you. You don't feel the same amount of confidence in what you are saying, and does it sound the same exhibiting the same amount of confidence you were feeling a few moments later.

If you have watched courtroom drama movies, you might have witnessed that lawyers easily intimidate the people sitting in the questioning box. Those people in the witness boxes might have been coached by their lawyers thoroughly. They've had coaching and assurances, yet their confidence crumbles in front of the lawyers.

Therefore, it is imperative to understand that overall body language plays an equally important role in making you more convincing.

It would be helpful to understand that as per studies, the contribution of your body language in the communication can be as high as 55%. It is not what we say that matters so much, but how we say that matters.

We'll now touch some important parts of your body language that display confidence.

> **Posture:** Your posture while you talk is very important. When you are talking, you must hold your head straight. Your spine and your head should remain in alignment. While talking, it is always better to keep your chin bent a little downwards. Hunching on the table or hanging your head while you talk are signs of weakness, fear, insecurities, and shame. Most people do not have control over their posture when they are nervous. It is nothing uncommon. However, you can practice your posture in front of someone you trust and visualize the difference and take mental notes to keep correcting your posture. Also, you need to remember that while you keep your spine erect and your head straight, you must not make your body stiff. Such a posture is difficult to hold for long, and as you begin slouching, you'll lose steam. Therefore, you must keep your body relaxed.

Placement of Hands: Placement of hands is also equally important. Confident people always have their hands visible. Never shove your hands inside your pockets as that would display your discomfort that can alarm other people.

Gait: Walking is an important indicator of the confidence you carry. If you are walking cautiously, taking small steps, or keeping your eyes glued to the floor, it displays your lack of confidence. You must always walk with confidence and long steps keeping your eyes pointed towards your destination.

Eye contact: You must never avoid eye contact. You are talking to that person, and there is no way you can be invisible; therefore, you do not have a cause to avoid eye contact. Avoiding eye contact displays your lack of confidence and anxiety.

Facial Expressions: Facial expressions are the hardest to control because there is a reflex action taking place, and your emotions easily come on your face. However, there are some ways to appear confident at all times. Your smile is your biggest deception.

When you have a smile on your face, there is little space left for other emotions. But you must remain cautious with your smile too because smiling too much or even when it isn't needed can be a big give away. You must have a soft and confident smile on your face. Besides smiling, you must not do things like biting your lips, blinking rapidly, or the clenching of jaws as they can show your underconfidence.

Body Language: Body language is very important to reflect confidence. It is very hard to control if you aren't very confident, but some people have poor body language even if they are confident about the things they are saying. Things like keeping your arms crossed while you talk, tilted head, avoidance of eye contact, trying to shift your weight continuously, and tapping of the feet are a few things that can clearly exhibit your anxiety, impatience, and frustration.

You must avoid doing all such things to appear confident in your conversations.

Understanding and Carrying Out Non - Verbal Communication

Non - verbal communication is the subject that focuses on your body language to convey what you are feeling at that moment. Like we discussed in the previous point about the ways to display confidence through your body language, in the same way, you can also communicate your every mood to others.

For instance, if your lips are pursed, you are making steady eye contact without blinking your eye contact, and you have your hands on your hips, it would signify that you are convinced of something bad about the person in question and you have made up your mind. On the other hand, have your hand by your side or using them while talking and you are smiling, it would suggest that you are open to discussions and comfortable; hence there is no reason to feel alarmed.

Most people develop fixed features and body language, and that comes in the way of varied approaches they might want to take.

Your body language must signal approachability if you want others to feel comfortable talking to you, and you must remain attentive when talking to others.

Understanding and carrying out verbal communication

Verbal communication is the art of having interesting and involving conversations. Most people falter in verbal communications because people don't want to talk to them for long. They try to join ongoing conversations but find that people stop taking an interest in what they want to say or begin leaving that place.

It can happen and would happen if what you are saying is boring, and you are not allowing others to contribute but forcing your thoughts and ideas on others. In such a case, people only have two choices, first to leave the conversation and avoid confrontation or second, raise an argument that can easily escalate. Wise people generally choose the first option and get out of the conversation, leaving feeling left out.

You must ask yourself the pertinent question of whether people enjoy talking to you, or are you forcing yourself on them?

If a high number of people leave your conversation midway, then the chances are that you are forcing yourself on them.

There are three parts of an engaging conversation:

> Introduction of an interesting topic: No one likes to take part in a boring conversation in which there is nothing for them to contribute or know. If you want people to take an interest in your conversation, you must introduce topics that have some intrigue or mass to discuss. It is always expected to avoid leading topics that have their leanings to one side.
>
> Asking clear questions: You must always remember that it is a conversation, and hence it must always remain two - sided and not take the form of a monologue. If you want the conversations to be engaging, you must ask questions that are clear and may elicit a response. Dead questions that may not have a clear answer or ambiguous questions will only lead to awkward silences and ended conversations.

Listening to them attentively: You must pay equal attention to listening. We have discussed listening already, but this point cannot be reiterated enough times.

Assertiveness

Assertiveness is the final ingredient of this social skill. Assertiveness is the quality of being confident about what you are saying. You'll see it usually that either people are very passive when they talk, and they are ready to accept whatever the person in front of them is saying. Such people are either too timid or sycophants. They have no respect for what they are saying, and will never be able to take a stand because they lack the skill of presenting clear and convincing ideas.

Then some people are not ready to back down and move with a single point agenda to have their say. Although they are uber confidence and they may win that discussion, they'll lose people who are interested in listening to what they have to say.

Usually, people in positions of power like to show this assertiveness, and they know that the listeners have very few options to choose from in their case.

However, that doesn't make it good or correct.

Assertiveness should always be used as a seasoning on the meal. You must take a stand and put your points in front of everyone but agree to disagree. You must not move with the agenda to make every person in the conversation agree to what you are saying.

If you learn the art of taking the middle path, you'll find striking conversations very easy. Not only that, but people would also agree to talk to you even on those topics they know your position is not on your side.

You must always keep in mind that people have a right to disagree with you, and you can't hold that against them. If people have even a little doubt that you'll try to make your point and make it a debate in case they do not agree to what you are saying, they might avoid the conversation altogether.

Social skills are necessary skills that have to be learned. You should not have the misconception that just because someone speaks good, that person has a special gift that you have been denied. You might have lacked the opportunity and exposure at some point, but it isn't the skill that you lack. The only thing you need is a little guidance and a lot of practice. You must keep that in your mind that you can't develop social skills without interacting with people. But, if you try, there is nothing that can stop you from having excellent social skills.

SECTION II
EVERYTHING BEGINS BY UNDERSTANDING THE MIND

CHAPTER 6: FEAR AND ANXIETY - THE FAMED FOES

Fear and anxiety are the familiar foes that most people with poor social skills experience. As soon as you are about to encounter a situation you aren't comfortable dealing with, you'll have a sudden surge of anxiety and fear within you. The feeling can be gut - wrenching. You will have an avoidance impulse that may provoke you to devise a strategy to get out of that situation.

You can have these feelings when you are about to:

- Meet or interact with someone intimidating or very powerful
- Facing a crowd or a group of people and the spotlight is upon you
- Confront someone very assertive or forceful
- Presenting an idea to influential or knowledgeable people

These are only some of the situations. People can have this feeling even when they are about to talk to someone new or asking for some favor.

Aborting the whole idea begins to look so much attractive all of a sudden.

In such a circumstance, people generally choose one of the three ways to dodge the bullet:

1. Total Avoidance: They avoid going to such places or meeting such people
2. Bailing Out: It is another approach. If such people can't avoid going, they try to find an excuse to get out of that situation
3. Prevent Interaction: In case bailing out isn't an option, they try to keep a low profile and keep a low profile, so they don't come in the spotlight

Such people would try to avoid meeting new people, approaching strangers, or discussing things that can lead to debates or may require them to take a stand

You may understand these situations and reactions very well because they are not uncommon. The problem is with the cause of these emotions.

Fear and anxieties are not external emotions. It is your mind that creates these emotions. You might have seen some people jump at the sight of roaches, rodents, and certain reptiles. There are millions of people in the world who might not feel anything looking at those creatures, and some even might like to have them in their plates.

Those tiny creatures can't cause that much fight. You know it very well that a roach can't cause any harm to you physically, yet some people who might get at their wits end by the mere sight of a roach while the poor fellow is trying to save its life.

It is not anything else that's causing that fear and anxiety within you, but your mind is making you feel so. Id it has a perception that something is dangerous, as soon as it spots that thing, it creates the same level of anxiety within you to make you feel fearful. It is a natural response to make you more aware and alert so that you can think of an escape route much before that thing becomes a real threat.

Fear and anxiety are natural mechanisms that have evolved over millions of years of the evolution process. They are not evil. The only bad thing is that although we have very few things that threaten our lives to the same extent, we are still fearful.

People with poor social skills have this fear in their minds about facing the crowds. They are always fearful that everybody in public would be looking at them and judging them about their appearance, behavior, and performance.

The Spotlight Effect

In the year 2000, professor Thomas Gilovich of Cornell University tried to evaluate this behavior. He carried out a study to identify the reasons for this kind of behavior and called it the 'spotlight effect.'

He formed groups of students and then randomly selected one student from each group. The rest of the students from each group then went to their classes. The professor made each student sit in a way that everyone was directly facing the door.

He intentionally kept the selected students engaged in something trivial so that they couldn't go to the class on time. He then asked those students to wear some t - shirts with a picture of famous personalities. It made them look different from other students.

He then asked those singled out students to go to their respective classes knowing fully well that they were late and also knowing that other students would be looking directly at them.

The objective of the experiment was to invoke the feeling of embarrassment in the respective students. It would help if you kept in mind that these students might not be dealing with any social anxiety or fear. They were random students selected from a group.

However, these students knew that they were late, and the professor made sure that they knew that when they'd enter the class, everyone would be looking directly at them.

So every selected student went to the class feeling responsible for being late and faced the whole class as the gate opened. They had those t - shirts on with a picture of a famous personality that made them stand out.

Once the experiment was over, the professor asked those students to think of the percentage of students who might have remembered their entry and presence vividly.

Those students believed that at least 50% of the students in the class would have clearly remembered them. They were sure that everyone was looking at them when they entered the classroom. They were confident that at least half of the students in the class would remember the image on their t - shirts as they were the focus of attention of the whole classroom.

The professor then asked every student in the various classrooms, which were a part of this study. He found that only less than 10 percent of the student in the class paid any real attention to the student and remembered that incident. Very few students paid attention to the image on the t - shirt worn by students entering late in the classroom as they never really paid that much attention to it.

This study found out that only 10 percent of students were able to remember the incident by the end of the class, and the number of students who could recall the image on the t - shirt was even less.

However, the students who were subjects of the study were sure that at least 50 percent of the students must have remembered them correctly.

This effect is called the spotlight effect. The study concluded that we all place too much importance on ourselves than others do, and that's why we are more conscious of our appearance and conduct.

The world cares much less about our presence as it is busy thinking about itself.

The world doesn't care much about our positive or negative aspects until it begins to affect them. It is futile to think that the spotlight is always upon you. Such a perception is always going to make you feel miserable. The more carefree you are about the reaction of others, the more confident you'll become.

This experiment proves that although we may keep worrying about what others might think about us, the world doesn't give two hoots about us as it has enough of its worries. It is not the world against you, but your mind that's making you feel conscious, fearful, and anxious.

People with poor social skills need to get this clear in their minds that it isn't the world that they have to deal with but their minds. The war of perception is going on within you, and the world doesn't hold you in the prime spot.

CHAPTER 7: THE CORRECT WAY TO BEGIN - IMPROVING YOUR SOCIAL SKILLS

Blame shifting is the biggest enemy most people have. We never look within us to find the real cause of our failure in anything. We like to find easy targets that can take the blame and shift the spotlight from us. We want to take a dip in the sympathy wave not because we need sympathy, but because it isn't accusatory.

It is a fact that if you are not very social, you may lack social skills. It has nothing to do with your proficiency, but it the art of practice. The more you practice, the more proficient you become.

However, a lack of practice is evident in people with poor social skills. If you try to know the cause, they'll quickly shift the blame to various things like:

- They lack the motivation to practice their social skills. Although the lack of motivation is only a façade, they like to play with it for the sake of face - saving.

- They feel social interactions are draining. They aren't faking it. When they have to interact with others, they feel as if they are dealing with something highly stressful.
- They try to console themselves by saying that they don't even like interacting with people, and hence there is no need to bother about working on social skills anyway.
- They genuinely believe that most people are not worth their attention and time. They only bring up painful things, and it is better to stay away from them.
- People like to consider bullying or other traumatic events in the past as an excuse to avoid people and social gatherings.
- People have a firm belief that several challenges are acting against them. Issues like mild autism, strutting, and Asperger's syndrome and similar physical limitations are definitive challenges that have curtailed their ability to have good social skills and confidence while talking to others.

If you also hold a similar viewpoint, it will be heartening for you to know that you are wrong. Most of the things that appear as limitations are just self -

imposed restrictions that will remain in place until you make an effort to lift them.

It isn't the world draining your energy or people talking nonsense that do that. The world is still full of life, vigor, and sense, and full of millions and millions of people who are making sene, or else the world would be in practically terrible shape.

The real problem lies in the fact that you are afraid to tackle the challenges that are preventing you from developing social skills. You are trying to look away while the solution is within your reach.

We'll now discuss these issues in detail:

Dealing with Lack of motivation

Lack of motivation is a serious issue that you will need to deal with complete sincerity. Most people with poor social skills generally do not show any intent in mixing with others. They are consciously trying to avoid interaction and even make desperate attempts at remaining inconspicuous. However, can you term that as a lack of motivation?

It isn't a lack of motivation but a dangerous mix of anxiety and internal resistance to change. Generally, people try to avoid socialization as they don't want the spotlight to get focused on them. They feel anxious at the thought that they'd have to deal with others, and their perception of themselves might get challenged. They have been living within themselves for such a long period that now any change can challenge them to break free of the patterns they have been following.

Therefore, it is not the motivation that such people lack, but there is an excess of anxiety and resistance to change that's making them feel so.

Does that mean they really can't have something to motivate them to change their attitude?

A motivated individual always has a goal in mind, and that helps in keeping the individual go. Without proper motivation, developing social skills can become very difficult. It is the primary force that'll make you venture out. It helps you improve.

Lack of motivation can kill all your aspirations ever to gain social skills. Every failure or embarrassment on the path will look like a roadblock that you'll find very difficult to overcome.

If you want to feel motivated to develop your social skills:

You will have to learn to deal with your anxieties: Anxiety may only be a single word, but it contains a dark and dangerous world within it. There are no quick fixes to anxiety disorders, but if you try to get over your anxieties, it is a possible feat. Fears and anxieties originate within our minds. They are a reaction to someone or something that you don't like very much or dislike for that matter. It also limits your familiarity with that object or person.

Dealing with anxiety would require you to understand your fears and apprehensions with better clarity. As we saw in the spotlight effect experiment, our perception of things might be completely different from that of the world. It is very much possible, and you do not have any way to know that until you explore that for yourself.

Fear of rejections, embarrassments, and failures can keep people feeling anxious. However, even if you remain in that state for years, there will be no solution at hand. The only way is to address this fear is to gather courage and try.

Acknowledge and accept your shortcomings: Nobody knows your flaws better than you. The world can only revise them. It can't be worse than it is at the moment.

Famous Tyrion Lannister of Game of Thrones once says these golden words, 'Never forget what you are. The rest of the world will not. Wear it like armor, and it can never be used to hurt you.'

These words may be from a TV series, but they have a precious lesson hidden in them. We are usually afraid to venture out because we are continuously trying to hide our shortcomings from the world.

Maybe you do not want to speak out because you stutter. You don't want to embarrass yourself in front of others. But do you think that people around you don't know that? By keeping quiet, you are depriving yourself of presenting your viewpoint that may be of equal importance. If you don't speak, people know that you stutter, and you are weak. If you talk, people would know your opinion, and they already knew that you stammer, and hence it isn't going to change anything. People may even appreciate the fact that you spoke and presented your idea.

The day you accept your shortcomings, they'll stop causing anxiety in front of the world.

Bring clarity in your mind: We wish like kids. We don't know what we'll do with the things we hope for, but we want to have them anyway. The case with developing social skills is not any different. However, such aspirations don't last very long because you begin to contemplate the futility of the gains as soon as you encounter roadblocks.

It is always better, to begin with only those objectives in mind that you wish for desperately. If you face problems in presenting your ideas in the office meetings, start working on that aspect alone. It will keep you focused and also prevent wastage of energy in other areas that are not your prime focus and might get you discouraged. For example, giving presentations and talking to random people in pubs require different skill sets. However, failing in any of these could get you intimidated to try either of them in the future.

Therefore, you must select your first objective carefully. Once you begin to feel confident in that, you'll feel inspired to explore other avenues, and you'll have your success to back you up.

Don't be hesitant of the first step: Martin Luther King once said, 'You don't have to see the whole staircase; just take the first step.' It is excellent advice when it comes to starting anything new in life.

When we are thinking of doing anything, we remain fixated on the goal. The goal is sometimes so far that we begin to lose hope even before we have started.

It is always better to take a little bit of risk and begin without thinking much about the consequences. Opening up with others is not such a risk that you will have to ponder that much or do a high - level risk analysis.

You may falter here and there, but you'll realize that you're not doing as poorly as you thought you'd perform. The first step is something every individual owes to himself or herself. You can't hope of reaching anywhere if you don't even take the first step.

Set Smaller Milestones: A big mistake that many people commit is setting larger goals. It is always useful to aim higher, but if you have acrophobia, even the thought of skydiving can make you dizzy.

Why not begin your journey by climbing something smaller and build your confidence from there.

Do not just set an intimidating goal but also have smaller milestones in the way that keep you reminding that you are making progress.

Please do not make it look any more difficult than it is: Overthinking is a sin that most people with poor social skills commit. They have all the time at their hands that they save by not mixing with others, and they misuse this time contemplating the consequences of their failure in their attempts.

Social interactions are not challenges. It is something we do on an everyday basis. You must always remember that people are not going to remember even if you failed once or twice at what you are trying to do. They have enough worries of their own.

If you remain obsessed thinking about it, you'll carry more pressure than you should, and it won't be healthy.

Try to keep it as light as you can. If possible, try to enjoy your social interactions. Do not try to take long strides, and you'll not have all the pressure on you, all at once.

The day you begin enjoying your little interactions, there'll be nothing that would stop you from exploring further.

Easing the Pressure

Doing something against your nature or habit is always difficult and draining. That's why interacting with people or facing others can be a very draining experience for the people struggling with their social skills.

Does that mean they should give up?

No, it doesn't. However, reality states otherwise. Most people with poor social skills feel extreme pressure on themselves, trying to interact with others. It is a reason they try to avoid such interactions. However, they also realize the cost of this avoidance.

There is no reason to get intimidated by pressure and anxiety buildup within you. It is essential to understand that you are not the only one facing these issues—most people who are trying to open up to the world face these pressures. It is normal to feel drained and tired early on in such interactions.

The trick is to devise ways to tackle these experiences wisely.

Quick Fixes:

Keep yourself energized: If you are at a social gathering and talking to people is making you feel drained, you can try taking short breaks and have coffee or some energy drink to regain your energy back. It is a standard solution we try for most draining situations, and it'll work just fine here too.

Do not give up too soon: There would be instances when you'll feel that dip in your energy levels, and you might feel tempted to leave. However, even the feelings of tiredness and energy drain are not permanent. They'll keep coming and going. If you give yourself some time, you'll find yourself in a better position to cope with the situation at hand.

Try to find interesting avenues of engagement: Boredom is one of the most significant precursors of lethargy. Once you start feeling bored, you may not find any incentive to engage. However, that can be a flawed approach to look at things. Try to find something that can interest you more, and staying there would become more manageable.

Long - term Changes in Approach:

Increase your exposure: It is no secret that at places you don't feel comfortable, you will only feel a rapid energy drain. Those places are not the cause of this feeling of discomfort but your low exposure to such events. A better way to feel more at home is to increase your exposure to such places. Try to push yourself to be at such events more often so that this discomfort goes away soon. Once you get accustomed to such sites, you'd find it easy to find your flow because you won't be evading the scene but finding ways to assimilate.

Find less disconcerting activities: Even if social gatherings look intimidating to you, not everything there can be equally troublesome. A few things are always there can you may find more interesting. Try to look for such things and keep yourself distracted and entertained by them. It is an easy way to get that feeling of uneasiness out of your mind.

Even if public discussions terrify you, not every topic can be equally dull or intimidating. You can try to take discussions in that direction and become a contributor to that discussion.

Practice, Practice, and Practice: There is no better substitute to practice. In the beginning, the same things that looked incredibly tough may begin to look comfortable and doable. It doesn't happen by magic, but it is a result of practice.

There are certain uneasy circumstances that you don't want to face. Yet, if you have to face them once in a while, they shake you from the core. But, imagine having to do that again and again.

While in school, most students never get called to the principle's office, and when they get called, the walk is always harrowing. However, think of those that get called almost daily. You'll see no anxiety on their face because they are familiar with the scenario and the consequences. They do not feel intimidated. They do that feel the same kind of churning in their belly.

Now, pay a little attention to the facts. Going once in a lifetime or going to the same place every day doesn't change the fact that you have to go to the principle's office. But, simply because you are familiar with the whole sequence takes the fear and feeling of discomfort out of the equation.

It is the magic of practicing facing such uncomfortable circumstances, repeatedly.

Begin with a little support: There should be no shame in learning to walk with the help of crutches. Almost everyone practices the same way. Interacting with strangers or with a group of highly intimidating people can be a harrowing experience for someone beginning to practice. However, that wouldn't remain the same if you've had prior practice with people you've known or trust.

If you find it uncomfortable to begin with real - life scenarios, there should be no shame in practicing talking to the people you know. It will give you the feel and make you comfortable in the experience.

Once you gain confidence with known people, try to expand the group and include people who might be unfamiliar, and then moving on to real - life settings can be easy.

Addressing the Inner Inhibitions

Terming others as undeserving of your time and attention is yet another easy escape route adopted by people to avoid dealing with their anxieties and poor social skills. They have almost convinced themselves that they either don't like interacting with others or socializing in popular terms or don't even like people at all.

Everyone can have an opinion. You are entitled to your opinion. However, when you have such a pessimist opinion about people around you, it is going to come back to sting you.

You are not living under a rock for sure. As long as you are living in society, you can't live in hiding forever. Social interactions are a must and not an option.

You don't have a choice in meeting or not meeting people; that's almost unavoidable. You have a choice of feeling uncomfortable every time you meet anyone or not feeling uncomfortable.

If you have poor social skills, you are going to feel miserable every time you have to interact with others. You know that for the fact that it's unavoidable. We live in an interdependent society, and most of the things are interlinked. From earning your bread and butter to availing various services, social contact is unavoidable.

Therefore, the whole argument that you don't like interacting with people doesn't hold water. It is not whether you like them or not but do they reciprocate or not. If you are uncomfortable in dealing with people, you will keep feeling awkward and also communicate that to others.

It is essential to understand that these are the excuses people use to hide their discomfort and inability to interact with others. They can also devise several other defenses like they don't have the kind of time required for socialization, or they lack the patience to bear the stupidity of others. Some people are honest, but they don't shy away from leaning on the pessimist side and form a belief that they don't have what it takes to be social. As per their understanding, they are a lost cause.

It is imperative to understand that developing social skills is neither challenging nor optional. It is a fundamental skill that you must possess if you want to lead a healthy, productive, and comfortable life. If you show a little persistence and patience, you'll realize that social skills would come naturally.

If you truly believe that:

- You do not feel like mixing with others
- You do not have the kind of time needed for developing social skills

- You do not have what it takes to develop social skills

You are probably trying to hide your inability to interact with others, and you have built a façade to hide the embarrassment.

Social interactions make us feel better. They help us feel more lively and protected. People around you can help by sharing your sorrows and increasing your happiness. Usually, it isn't your lack of interest in socializing, but your inability to be social that comes in the way.

As you know, developing social skills is a continuous process; several smaller initiatives can also help you in becoming comfortable.

You can begin your journey of developing social skills by:

Try to find chances to meet people as often as possible: One of the biggest impediments people face in the path of social skill development is the lack of exposure. They meet people so less that they are never able to develop that level of familiarity and frankness. Social skill is all about developing relationships, and they require your time. You can't expect yourself to become socially proficient by venturing out once in a year or by talking to your coworkers once in a blue moon.

Learning social skills is like learning any other necessary skill. It is not just a people - pleasing skill but a survival skill. You can look around, and you'll find there are several settings in which you can survive without other vital skills like swimming, driving, or even computer skills. Still, you won't be able to survive without social skills, even for a brief period, and never thrive at all.

You must have seen several people cribbing around you about missed promotions and opportunities. Several people think that they could have given a better presentation or explained something better to the client. Yet, the chance went to someone else.

Do you think it is always sycophancy that does the trick, and you can completely discredit that person?

The reality is harsh and bitter, but it is the reality. You lose such chances because you sat at your place, wishing for that opportunity. At the same time, someone else had taken the initiative to present his/her skills. It certainly requires a certain degree of familiarity and frankness, and you can get that if you become a little more sincere in your attempt to venture out and socialize. You won't find yourself out of place and alien.

Become an efficient time - manager: Socializing takes time. You can't do that while you are busy with your computer screen or in your files. It definitely takes time and effort that you'd need to find. If you feel that you run on a hectic schedule and you don't have that time, then you aren't looking properly. Generally, people can't be busy all the time, every time. Even if you have a lot of things on your hands, try to manage them more efficiently so that you can find time to socialize.

Look for the open spots: It is also an extension of the previous point. In case you really can't find a lot of time to meet people or have time to socialize, you must try to schedule things in a way that allows you to meet people within your schedule.

For instance, if you have a meeting scheduled at a particular location, try to meet your friends available in that direction. It'll save your traveling time, and you'll also be able to meet someone you haven't met in a long - time.

Focus on quality: Your focus must not go away from the objective of these socializations, and that is to increase your exposure and make you feel comfortable in social gatherings and public places. You can only achieve it when you are indulging in the right kind of activities. If you are meeting friends and spend all the time watching movies or playing games, there will be no real interaction. In place of that, try to meet people and discuss things and practice free - flowing conversations on a wide range of topics.

Make it fun and team activity: In the end, anything that's fun is always more attractive and engaging. It motivates you to try something like that again. If you can find ways to make your social interactions more fun and full of enjoyable activities, it'd be much easier for you to loosen your inhibitions and open up in a real sense. You can plan outings with your friends or other fun activities and get better exposure to other people while you are not even feeling vulnerable.

These are some of the ways that can help you in overcoming your inhibitions. Breaking the cocoon of social alienation is not an easy task. It is not going to happen overnight. It is not going to happen without hiccups. But, it is also not going to happen if you don't make sincere attempts.

Dealing with Bullying and Traumatic Past

There are a few things in life over which we have no control, and yet they affect our lives profoundly. Bullying, molestation in the past, sexual harassment, or any other kind of traumatic event can scar anyone's life forever. Such events are beyond our control, but it can't be reasonable to hold them as an excuse to remain locked in your shell.

Some people are evil. That doesn't make the whole humanity corrupt. Until you venture out and try to know people, you'll never be able to realize the good within them.

Bullying: It is terrible to bully anyone. Yet, some people bully others. People can face bullying for a wide range of things. Some people get bullied even for the things over which they have no active control, like their race, color, height, and ethnicity. If you have been bullied on such issues, there is nothing that you need to change within you. The problem is not within you but in them. Yet, you can't take anything said by people on its face value.

There can be things that you might think that you lacked, and people picked on you for those things. You can definitely work on those things to get over the feeling of inferiority within you.

While we can never hold the victim responsible for any bullying, even for the victim, it isn't healthy to wear victimhood as an excuse to keep bearing the pain and continue living in fear.

You will have to attempt to break free of the shackles of such fears and overcome them. Developing social skills and facing the world head - on is the best way to do this.

Traumatic events in the past: Like bullying, there is nothing that you can do about something terrible that might have happened in the past. However, it can never be prudent to allow that horrible incident to rule your life and all your future decisions.

Good social skills provide you an opportunity to get out in the world and explore new people who can give you a better perspective of this world and the way it functions. Undeniably, there would be several people who are mean, unfair, and even terrible. Still, you also can't ignore that there would be a lot more people who are generous, polite, helpful, loving, and caring.

All you'd need is to look out for such people and remain watchful of the people around you. Good social skills help you in mixing with people and knowing them better so that you can make an informed choice.

Learning to Work with Your Challenges

Physically challenges are beyond our control. Some people may stutter and feel disadvantaged. They have a right to feel so. However, even if they keep feeling victimized, it isn't going to improve their situation.

It is a fact that physical disadvantages like stammering, autism, Asperger's syndrome, etc. put people in disadvantageous positions. They might not feel the same amount of confidence.

Do you know the story of Nick Vujicic?

He is an acclaimed Australian painter, swimmer, skydiver, and motivational speaker in his late 30's.

He has given over 3000 talks in more than 57 countries. Some of his talks have had as many as 110,000 people in the audience.

Nick was born with a rare congenital condition called Phocomelia. People with this condition are born without limbs. He didn't have hands or feet since birth. I'd request you to let all that sink in with the context of him being a painter, swimmer, skydiver, and motivational speaker.

Now imagine a limbless person doing all that.

Terming Nick's journey as just difficult would be an injustice. He was bullied and attempted suicide even when he was merely ten years old. Think of the mental, emotional, and physical pain he might have endured at that tender age without any hope of betterment in the future. Yet, that made him more determined, and he turned his life around.

I'd only like to put one question to you.

Are you at an even more disadvantageous position than Nick Vujicic that you can't turn your life around?

SECTION III
IMPROVING CONVERSATION SKILLS

CHAPTER 8: THE CORRECT WAY TO BEGIN - IMPROVING YOUR SOCIAL SKILLS

Until now, we've had a thorough discussion about the causes of poor social skills in some individuals and the main areas they should focus on bringing improvement.

We've also discussed at length the main psychological impediments that such individuals face. Overcoming the mental barriers can be among the biggest challenges that you may have to overcome. It is not the world that scares us but our mind that fears the world. Once the mind learns the ways to overcome these challenges, the rest is just practice.

Like all the skills in the world, even social skills can be improved in a step by step manner. It is a systematic process, and hence if you pay attention, stick to the process, there is no reason for you not to make improvements.

This chapter onwards, we'll get into the nitty - gritty of developing social skills. We'll begin with the basics and understand what it takes to make conversations work. We'll also try to get to know the things that can stall conversations and make it difficult to have fruitful conversations flowing.

We can be as talkative as birds. However, every conversation is not fruitful and effective. Some will leave you with a bad taste in mouth while there will be others where you might feel that you overstepped your boundaries or even got humiliated. A conversation can result in all these scenarios and many more.

Being able to converse fluently can be one of the most crucial parts of social skills. It is indicative of your confidence, ability to process thoughts seamlessly, and the strength in your personality.

These three factors can have a deep impact on your conversations and will determine whether people like to engage with you or not.

Let us discuss all the three factors in some detail:

Overcoming Shyness and Anxiety: For any conversation to begin, you will need to overcome your shyness and anxiety. If you are feeling too anxious while beginning your conversations, your thoughts will get muddled, and the flow of information will get affected. It would help if you got into a conversation with confidence. Now, I understand that it is easier said than done. If you have been struggling with your social skills, gathering all that confidence, in the beginning, can be a tough task to manage. However, you can allow the conversation to pick up its pace and then join in with better inputs. It can be tough if only two people are talking, as it can lead to awkward silences. In such a case, it is always better to initiate with some small talk and then get to a specific topic of common interest.

Too much anxiety, shyness, and overthinking can lead to confused thoughts, and hence you must avoid those at all costs. You do not need to be anxious. It is only a conversation that will end anyway one way or the other. There is no need for you to panic or overprepare. You are not going to take an exam.

Conversation Skills: This part is purely technical. Once the conversation has begun, your inputs will depend completely on your ability to form thoughts and put relevant facts in perspective.

Most people make a drastic mistake here. They are only interested in speaking their minds and do not pay attention to what others are saying or the feelings of others.

A conversation takes only a bit to turn into an argument if it isn't conducted correctly.

If you want to be good at conversations and want people to appreciate what you say, you must pay attention to what others have to say. Listening is a superpower we all have but seldom utilize.

The next thing is empathy. While the purpose of a conversation is to make others aware of your thought and get to know more about things, it isn't a war of ideologies. There can be differences in opinions, and you must respect them. You must also empathize with others and try to understand their viewpoint if you want the conversations to be fruitful.

Your body language also plays a major role in conversations. If you are not exhibiting confidence through your body language, you might have to work extra hard to get the point across.

Last but not least is your knowledge of the subject. Some people have to speak no matter what the subject of discussion is. If you want to develop your social skills, you don't have to be that person who is eager to speak merely for the sake of speaking.

Whatever you say must be relevant to the topic and concise. It is always better to speak for an effect and not only because you want yourself to be heard.

Your Stance: It is a fact that conversations bring out the personality of the speakers. Some people speak with a single point program to prove their point. They don't want to admit the fact that even others could be wrong. If the conversation is not going their way, they can be offensive and aggressive. Some people are meek, and they'd agree to anything that others have to say.

Being able to put forth your opinion is one thing, but being argumentative is entirely something different. It is a negative trait that you must avoid. Such people not only have very few people to converse with but can also easily offend many people.

It would help if you always remembered that holding a good conversation is a skill that you learn one step at a time. It isn't something that you can master in your first attempt.

There will be conversations where you'll have people with whom you'd want to keep on talking forever. However, there can also be conversations that might not go well. You'll have to accept both as you can't choose them before they begin. Any specific type of conversation shouldn't intimidate you or make you feel underconfident.

Another important thing is to understand that every individual is different when it comes to holding conversations. It would be best if you didn't try to copy someone or feel jealous about someone else's conversation skills. You must keep working on your skills and try to become more confident.

CHAPTER 9: ADAPT TO BECOME THE RIGHT PERSON FOR HAVING MEANINGFUL CONVERSATIONS

You'd usually find people fretting over the fact that they don't get the right kind of people to talk to or most people are very boring. If you have also been struggling with your social skills, even you might have witnessed that most people that you come across don't really have anything interesting to talk about in their conversations. They keep talking as if playing on a loop.

Have you ever tried to notice the fundamental problems in their conversations?

We all make mistakes, and then we learn from those mistakes. However, it is a fact that this life is too short for committing all the mistakes to learn lessons. You can also learn from the mistakes committed by others.

The biggest mistake most people make in their conversations is that they never appear to be as interesting as they should be. It doesn't mean to be offensive, but if there is nothing in the conversation for you, there may not be an incentive to bear it for long. It is the simple concept on which conversations work.

Highly talkative people or extroverts can manage this shortcoming by talking to a lot more people and having a lot to talk about and discuss. However, that may not be possible for an introvert person or a person with poor social skills or a very limited social exposure.

Conversations require all the participants to invest their time and attention into the conversation. For the sake of courtesy, any person engaged by you can be physically present in the conversation, not to appear offensive or rude. If you look back, you might have done the same countless times. However, didn't you feel trapped and bored. People go on talking about routine things of their interest without paying attention to the interest of the listener.

As a person working on your social skills, you don't have to be that kind of individual. This chapter will help you understand the ways to help you become an interesting person with whom people would enjoy having long conversations.

Try to find common ground: It is a problem that you might have experienced several times in your life. People strike conversations, and then without paying attention to your interest in that topic, they begin to rant about their concerns. It is a classic example of boring conversations.

Most conversations have a slow start like a steam engine. It takes some time for the steam to build the pressure to begin pushing the engine hard. At the same time, if you begin behaving like an electric engine ready to shoot the moment the engine is fired, it can take the other person by surprise.

People take some time to warm up and find common ground for discussion. If you want to be a person who can hold long and interesting conversations, you'll need to learn the art to make people comfortable with some small talk and then find a common topic of interest that you can discuss.

You must understand the vital difference between a conversation and a monologue. If you are the only one talking, and the other participant is only standing mute, nodding, or adding yes or no to the conversation. The conversation is definitely headed into the direction of being a monologue. It wouldn't last long, and it'd not have a high satisfactory value.

Every conversation must begin with a warm - up where all the participants become familiar with each other. They'd definitely begin sending signals whether they are getting bored or would like to continue.

After this stage, you'll need to test a common topic of interest. For instance, you may have a few interesting things to talk about the current state of politics. However, most people don't like to talk about their political opinion in public as the discussions easily flare - up. They like to keep their ideologies to themselves or discuss them only with likeminded people. Forcibly probing such a topic would be an intrusion in privacy.

It is always better to find a topic of common interest as you'd be able to have a good conversation on a positive note if both of you know about that topic, as well as have an interest in it.

If you could find such a topic of conversation, not only this conversation, but even future conversations with that person would be very productive even if they are not on the topics of common interest.

When you have a lengthy discussion with a person cordially, it helps in the development of personal rapport that lowers inhibitions, and not only you, but even others open up to you.

Some people feel that trying to know the common interests and feelings may look invasive and offensive. It won't if you are polite and not very direct. Asking questions about things like common interests, passions, and experiences gives the other person a chance to be more open. All you'd need to do after than is to put follow up questions to get deep insights.

The more the conversations are based on the follow up of experiences and interests of the other person, the more interesting they'll get.

Don't try to be the central theme of the conversations: There should be no shame in admitting the fact that our minds are overly focused on ourselves. When you are watching a movie, the mind likes to put you in the place of the protagonist. It is the reason everyone roots for the protagonist to win. Every individual in his/her mind is central to every problem and solution.

There is nothing wrong with that because this is how our minds have been hardwired. However, most people learn to understand the roles they play in reality and never overstep their boundaries. It is a rule mostly overlooked in conversations.

Most of the time, our conversations are primarily focused on us. As you can understand, the other person may feel bored or uncomfortable in such conversations.

If you are trying to engage others in the conversation, encourage them to talk about themselves. When people get a chance to talk about themselves or place their opinion, they feel comfortable and retain a positive memory of the conversation. It also means that the next time you talk to them, they'll easily be able to recall you as a better person to talk to, and it can be a big boost to your social skill development.

Keeping others involved: It invariably happens that one person becomes dominant in conversations due to a better grip on the topic or relevance. It can make conversations monotonous and boring. If you are in control of the conversation in such a way, it'd be better if you keep the others involved by taking their inputs.

Even in general, it is always a good idea to keep others involved by ending your sentences in questions. It gives you a unique advantage of getting a response from others, and you can also keep them engaged.

At the end of your sentences, you can ask for their thoughts or opinions and advice on the matter. It makes the other people in the conversation feel involved. When you ask anyone for their advice, it naturally fills them with the feeling of significance, and it is always a positive feeling. It is again a good way to leave a positive impression on the mind of the listeners.

Body language is important: We've already discussed the importance of body language in communications. If your body language is positive and confident, you can disarm and charm the people you are talking to and get better engagement.

A genuine and sparkling smile is contagious, and it can make others smile too. If you want people to enjoy the conversations, never let that genuine smile go away from your face. No matter the context of the conversation, a smile can help others feel comfortable.

At the same time, you must also keep a note of the body language of the other people involved in the conversation. Body language can give you an idea of whether they are open for discussion or they are feeling tensed or bored.

Body language forms 55 percent of the entire conversation, and hence the unsaid holds much more significance than the said things in a conversation. If you ignore the importance of body language, you may hold people longer than they'd like to remain tied to the discussion, and that may not be very healthy for future discussions.

Before you comment about the unsuitability of others for a good conversation, you must look inside and evaluate whether you are the kind of person with whom people would like to have long conversations.

Changing your mindset and adapting yourself is all it takes to become a person with whom others would like to have genuine conversations that can flow freely and have a healthy outcome.

CHAPTER 10: COMING OUT OF THE SILENCE ZONE

Learning new things is a great thing, but the practical application of those things, especially social skills, is a very challenging task. Most people know what they'd like to say; they have the whole script in mind; some may have even rehearsed it a few times, but when the final moment comes to utter those words, they are at a loss of words.

It is the life struggle of most people who struggle with their social skills. They can be shy, introverts, and anxious people, but they aren't dumb. They have a lot of things to say that they think they know better than others. Yet, when the moment comes to speak, they are unable to come up with something intelligent enough in their minds, and hence they keep mum. If you are angry that it happens with you more often than you'd like to remember, you're not alone.

You are generally not struggling with what to say, but what would be the better argument at that point. The problem of choice arrests you.

Knowing what to say at that moment is your primary problem, and we'll discuss it at length.

Please do not make it a big deal: Most people who do not have a very higher engagement rate would like to make every engagement count. It is the reason they are always busy in their mind trying to come up with something very intelligent and engaging. You do not need to do that.

We want to say something very clever because we want to appear to be the best and think that everyone is going to pay great attention to it. Here, you need to understand that there is no need to attach so much attention to yourself.

We all like to believe that everyone is paying close attention to us, but we forget the spotlight effect. Our words and actions may not be that important for others as we may like to believe.

In your mind, the more you emphasize the attention you ought to receive from the conversation, the more pressurized and anxious you'll feel.

It would help if you learned to take t easy. The purpose of a conversation is not to establish your supremacy but to exchange ideas and discuss positive things.

The people who get the most attention in conversations are the ones who are very carefree. They keep the banter light and do not attach too much self-importance. It also makes others feel easy around them.

You can begin a conversation with anything you like. It is always better to have some small talk so that everyone can lower the guards.

You don't need to appear as the most intelligent or important contributor as long as you can avoid being rude: We all wish to appear knowledgable and important. However, you do not need to keep searching for the right words until the end of the conversation. It is simply a conversation and not an exam.

As long as you do not appear rude, you do not need to worry even if you are not the brightest contributor to the conversation. You'll not turn the spotlight towards yourself until you have spoken something very offensive that leaves others rattled.

It is one thing to be a casual contributor and remain a normal part of the conversation and completely another to come in the spotlight for all the wrong reasons.

If you do not have something positive to add to the conversation, please pay attention to the things being said, and you may get something to present your views. It would help if you kept in mind that remaining positive and taking the conversation in the right direction is always better for everyone.

Take your time: Do not rush to say things. Take your time and find the key points where you could add something relevant and valuable. If you are still practicing your art of conversation skills, it is always better to be specific.

Do not begin adding anything to the conversation for the sake of it. Listen to the things being said and react to them as needed.

It's important to understand that you do not need to respond to everything verbally. Many times, the things said may require your reaction in the form of laughter or approval. You don't need to formulate your joke in reply. Appreciating something funny said in a conversation encourages others more.

If someone has added something important to the conversation, you can again appreciate that or try to know more about it, as that is also a way to show your encouragement and appreciation.

Be watchful and appreciative: Starting a new conversation can be tough for many people as they find themselves at the loss of words. A good way to begin is to be more watchful of your surrounding and be appreciative of it.

When you observe something in your surroundings and appreciate it, you may get a reply that has a positive tone. It is easier to carry such conversations forward.

Conversations leaning on the negative side tend to bring your critical and pessimist view outside even if that may not be your true nature.

Always pay attention to the things being said: It is a golden rule of conversations that most people overlook. Most people are very enthusiastic about the things they have to say, but when others are speaking, they don't pay close attention and get busy with other distractions like their phones.

It is a very bad thing to do on so many levels. First, because you are busy somewhere else, you may not be able to pay close attention to the things being said. It may make you wonder about the things to say next. Second, the person speaking to you may be observing you, and such an act might look offensive.

Therefore, every time you feel distracted by something else or even when your thoughts are diverted in some other direction in your mind, you must drag your awareness back to the discussion and try to get involved through follow up questions.

Be descriptive in your replies: Avoiding answers or trying to be quick with your replies is not good for your social skill development.

Questions will be directed towards you for your opinion or take on the matter. Most people like to take the quick route and pass the question with a concise yes or no.

It may not be the correct approach as you lose the opportunity to have an open discussion and present your views.

You do not need to drag the point but always try to present relevant information so that the listeners have enough data to evaluate.

Be a seeker: Conversations are for seekers. The people who want to enhance their understanding of things can have better conversations. If you believe that there is nothing more to know for you, then it is more likely that you'll become someone prepped for a debate. It happens because we always have that feeling of superiority of knowledge. It blocks our ability to grasp anything new.

If you want others to be interested in talking to you, you must become a person who is curious to know more. Always remember that no one likes to be evaluated on everything, and you'll be doing that if you think that you know everything.

A curious person is always the best to have fruitful conversations as such a person can help in bringing a new perspective. You don't need to fake this curiosity. Just be eager to listen, and you'll find several things that you may feel like exploring deeply.

Show genuine interest in people: It is another very important thing that can help you win brownie points in conversations. It would be best if you always remembered that everyone has a focus on the self. We may show interest in various things, but the end goal of the whole pursuit is the development of the self.

We really like it when someone shows a general interest in us and wants to know more about our viewpoint and us. It can even raise the curiosity of other people in the conversation in you. It is something very easy to reciprocate.

If you want to have people to take an interest in you, it is you who would have to show some interest in them. Do not try to fake your interest as that doesn't work.

People are full of new things, interests, and information. You only need to expand your horizon of interests, and you will find there is a lot to know.

Don't try to outwit others: We have a poor understanding of social recognition. We like to believe that if we have to remain relevant, we may have to appear as the smartest individual in the conversation.

When you are trying to have a deep conversation with others, try to be as real as you can. Do not focus too much on thinking the smartest thing to say that would impress other people. You can even impress them with your listening skills, your genuine interest in the conversation, or even your curiosity about that topic.

It is your warmth and understanding of the topic that would have a lasting impact and not the knowledge that you might possess.

What If You Hit a Wall

It is a real possibility that while having a conversation, you may hit a wall and not know what to say. There may be times when you may find yourself out of place in a contribution against the knowledge of other contributors.

Even such possibilities do take place once in a while. You can leave such conversations, and there is no need to feel out of place.

Remain appreciative, curious, and cheerful: It is a possibility that you may not feel that there is something new or useful that you can contribute. Does that give you a right to sit in a sullen mood or remain silent?

As we have discussed earlier, every person is reading the other, and your silence may not go unnoticed. You may appear to be moody, sulking, uninterested, or even disapproving. You cannot have a leash on the imagination of others.

You must maintain a positive demeanor and keep yourself involved in the conversation.

You may not find anything valuable to contribute to the conversation, but nothing can stop you from appreciating the good things being discussed. There may be several things that you might not have known; it can be one of the reasons you aren't able to contribute. You can express your curiosity to know more about such things and ask the followup questions.

Interest is a two - way street. You can only have the interest of others in you, as long as you are ready to reciprocate the same. Do not expect to get a warm reception while you show disregard to others.

Keen listening is also indicative of your participation: There would be times when you may not find anything productive to add to any conversation. Does that give you the right to indicate boredom?

You may reach this juncture in conversations, and this might happen very often in the beginning. You may feel that every other contributor has many valuable insights, or the topic of discussion is not of the area of your expertise. However, that makes it even more important for you to pay even closer attention to the things being said. You can gain more knowledge and insights.

Usually, this is not what happens. Most people begin to feel bored and lose all their interest in such conversations.

You may not have anything to add to the conversation, yet you can still contribute by listening keenly. You must remember that your body language is also a part of the conversation, and it can also convey your feelings. If you are keenly listening to the conversation, you will continue to hold the attention of the speakers.

Trust your instincts: Our instinct is very helpful when it comes to striking conversations. There will be times when you may not have a thorough knowledge of some subjects, and you may feel the gap. Lack of deep knowledge is an asset, but as long as it is an informal conversation and not a scientific discourse, it cannot be a prerequisite. You can say things or ask questions based on your instincts if you still want to participate.

When you are talking with your instinct, you must remember that you can't be rude or offensive. No one has the right to be rude or offensive in conversations, but some people with authority on the subject may sound imposing. However, you must always avoid crossing that line. Expressing an idea is always acceptable, but making people believe in that would require facts that you may not have at that moment.

CHAPTER 11: BEGINNING CONVERSATIONS

When it comes to striking a conversation, people generally find themselves at a loss of words. They know the standard salutations, but they know that the conversation might end in awkward silence or come to an abrupt end.

We meet people all the time, and although we want to strike a conversation, we always put that for later because we don't know the right thing to say.

A large part of the world population suffers from this issue, and therefore, you have no reason to sulk alone.

Now coming to the basic question, striking a conversation and taking it forward are two distinct things, but the second can't happen without the first.

You may have a plethora of good things to discuss with someone, but you will have to initiate the discussion and then take it forward to your desired destination.

No matter whether you are going to begin a conversation with a stranger or with an acquaintance, you'd require something relevant to talk about in the beginning.

Therefore, a proper beginning that doesn't let the conversation drop at that instant is very important. Then you'll need to know the way to carry the conversation in the intended direction without boring the other person. Finally, you must also know the ways to end the conversation positively so that it has the possibility of future discussions.

We'll discuss that in a step by step manner:

The Opening

Begin by asking something relevant to the situation: We grow up with simple introductions and salutations. Most of the people we know are our acquaintances, and hence there is no need for an introductory line. However, when it comes to starting a conversation with a stranger, things can be very different.

You have to ensure that you do not appear to be a creep or someone with mala fide intentions, and hence you must avoid asking direct or personal questions.

Asking something relevant to the situation like where you could get something that the person in question has or if that person could tell you something specific that you might not know.

For instance, if you are traveling, you can ask anything specific about the amenities available, the seating, or anything specific about the place you are going.

The person in question may not have the answer, but it will give you a chance to begin the conversation without looking like a creep or someone desperate.

Most of us fail to acknowledge the fact, but all of us are helpful beings. Helping others is an inherent quality that everyone has. You'll find very few people with a stone wall in front of their hearts, and hence the chances of getting a reply to such questions are much higher. Even the possibility of the conversation ending with abrupt silence is also low.

Do not worry about being unique with your opening lines: We all want to have something to say that may not have been told before. You could lose the opportunity to strike a conversation while you keep mulling over the line.

It isn't the opening line that you are going to discuss; hence there is no reason to fret over it. It may have been repeated, but if it is relevant, it will work.

A rather important thing to pay attention to at that moment is your ability to appear genuine, welcoming, and ingenious.

The eagerness and openness you demonstrate for the conversation will be the determining factor whether the conversation goes anywhere or drops dead after curt one - word replies.

Always pay attention to the body language: We live in a complex world where everyone is trapped within the problems floating in mind. There are times when people are eager to get out of these virtual issues and would reflect it through their body language, and there would also be times when people would want to stay there and not reciprocate well.

Much before they express that in words, such things would be visible through their body language, and you would have to monitor that.

Signs of mutual interest in the conversation are not hard to find. If you are trying to strike a conversation with someone and find that individual trying to look away and pointing feet away from you, it is a sign that the person is trying to avoid the conversation.

If the person is making eye contact with you often and has turned the direction of the feet toward you, it is a positive sign that the person is taking an interest in the conversation.

Taking Conversations Forward

Follow - up questions are crucial for an ongoing conversation: When you are talking to a person with no familiarity, the only way to know that person and keep the conversation going is through follow up questions. It also helps you in knowing that person better.

Follow up questions are an indication that you have an interest in the conversation, and you'd like it to continue. However, it would help if you remain careful in framing the follow - up questions, and some questions may not look appropriate.

Keep your follow up questions look like extensions of their previous reply and do not make them invasive. Keeping the questions focused on information in general and not making them directed as personal is always a good strategy.

Be open to sharing information about yourself: While you are primarily asking the questions and the follow - ups, you must keep in mind that it is an interaction and not an interrogation. You should also share information regarding you relevant to the answers provided by the other person.

For instance, if that individual has told about the place where he/she was brought up, you should also tell about the place you were brought up and any similarities or dissimilarities between the places.

Such an exchange of information always helps you in taking the conversation forward in a pleasant way.

There is an actual exchange of information taking place, and you have every reason to take the conversation forward.

Every follow - up information you get will give you a chance to put your bit and ask further questions.

You can extend the conversation easily and not feel it stretching a bit too long.

Keep conversations open - ended: Some questions have a defined reply, and then the conversations come to an end. However, you can also place questions in a way that they may remain open - ended and leave space for further inquiry. For instance, if you ask a person about the most liked or disliked place, the answer may come in one word and have no space for further inquiry; however, if you ask the same person about the last place, he/she would like to go ever in life and why, the answer will have a scope of details.

Keep your tone friendly and polite: Conversations are not interviews. It is a social exercise and not a test on which you are to be evaluated. You do not need to worry about being confident or imposing. All you need is a friendly tone, genuine warmth, and politeness.

Most people keep worrying about being very confident or assertive when they talk to someone. It is not the approach required to begin a conversation with a stranger.

It would help if you remained polite at all times and reflected a genuine interest in the conversation.

Bringing Conversations to an End

Express your gratitude with complete sincerity: Everything has to come to an end at some point in time, and conversations are no exception to a rule. However, they must not come to an abrupt end.

It would be best if you learned to express your gratitude while ending conversations. Thank the person genuinely for the time and valuable insights and express what you gained from the conversation.

We can do very little for people around us, but even a few words of gratitude can help people feel pleasant, satisfied, and valuable.

You can also expect the same to come back to you, and that would help in boosting your confidence for future conversations.

CHAPTER 12: BEGINNING CONVERSATIONS

When it comes to striking a conversation, people generally find themselves at a loss of words. They know the standard salutations, but they know that the conversation might end in awkward silence or come to an abrupt end.

We meet people all the time, and although we want to strike a conversation, we always put that for later because we don't know the right thing to say.

A large part of the world population suffers from this issue, and therefore, you have no reason to sulk alone.

Now coming to the basic question, striking a conversation and taking it forward are two distinct things, but the second can't happen without the first.

You may have a plethora of good things to discuss with someone, but you will have to initiate the discussion and then take it forward to your desired destination.

No matter whether you are going to begin a conversation with a stranger or with an acquaintance, you'd require something relevant to talk about in the beginning.

Therefore, a proper beginning that doesn't let the conversation drop at that instant is very important. Then you'll need to know the way to carry the conversation in the intended direction without boring the other person. Finally, you must also know the ways to end the conversation positively so that it has the possibility of future discussions.

We'll discuss that in a step by step manner:

The Opening

Begin by asking something relevant to the situation: We grow up with simple introductions and salutations. Most of the people we know are our acquaintances, and hence there is no need for an introductory line. However, when it comes to starting a conversation with a stranger, things can be very different.

You have to ensure that you do not appear to be a creep or someone with mala fide intentions, and hence you must avoid asking direct or personal questions.

Asking something relevant to the situation like where you could get something that the person in question has or if that person could tell you something specific that you might not know.

For instance, if you are traveling, you can ask anything specific about the amenities available, the seating, or anything specific about the place you are going.

The person in question may not have the answer, but it will give you a chance to begin the conversation without looking like a creep or someone desperate.

Most of us fail to acknowledge the fact, but all of us are helpful beings. Helping others is an inherent quality that everyone has. You'll find very few people with a stone wall in front of their hearts, and hence the chances of getting a reply to such questions are much higher. Even the possibility of the conversation ending with abrupt silence is also low.

Do not worry about being unique with your opening lines: We all want to have something to say that may not have been told before. You could lose the opportunity to strike a conversation while you keep mulling over the line.

It isn't the opening line that you are going to discuss; hence there is no reason to fret over it. It may have been repeated, but if it is relevant, it will work.

A rather important thing to pay attention to at that moment is your ability to appear genuine, welcoming, and ingenious.

The eagerness and openness you demonstrate for the conversation will be the determining factor whether the conversation goes anywhere or drops dead after curt one - word replies.

Always pay attention to the body language: We live in a complex world where everyone is trapped within the problems floating in mind. There are times when people are eager to get out of these virtual issues and would reflect it through their body language, and there would also be times when people would want to stay there and not reciprocate well.

Much before they express that in words, such things would be visible through their body language, and you would have to monitor that.

Signs of mutual interest in the conversation are not hard to find. If you are trying to strike a conversation with someone and find that individual trying to look away and pointing feet away from you, it is a sign that the person is trying to avoid the conversation.

If the person is making eye contact with you often and has turned the direction of the feet toward you, it is a positive sign that the person is taking an interest in the conversation.

Taking Conversations Forward

Follow - up questions are crucial for an ongoing conversation: When you are talking to a person with no familiarity, the only way to know that person and keep the conversation going is through follow up questions. It also helps you in knowing that person better.

Follow - up questions are an indication that you have an interest in the conversation, and you'd like it to continue. However, it would help if you remain careful in framing the follow up questions, and some questions may not look appropriate.

Keep your follow up questions look like extensions of their previous reply and do not make them invasive. Keeping the questions focused on information in general and not making them directed as personal is always a good strategy.

Be open to sharing information about yourself: While you are primarily asking the questions and the follow - ups, you must keep in mind that it is an interaction and not an interrogation. You should also share information regarding you relevant to the answers provided by the other person.

For instance, if that individual has told about the place where he/she was brought up, you should also tell about the place you were brought up and any similarities or dissimilarities between the places.

Such an exchange of information always helps you in taking the conversation forward in a pleasant way.

There is an actual exchange of information taking place, and you have every reason to take the conversation forward.

Every follow - up information you get will give you a chance to put your bit and ask further questions.

You can extend the conversation easily and not feel it stretching a bit too long.

Keep conversations open - ended: Some questions have a defined reply, and then the conversations come to an end. However, you can also place questions in a way that they may remain open - ended and leave space for further inquiry. For instance, if you ask a person about the most liked or disliked place, the answer may come in one word and have no space for further inquiry; however, if you ask the same person about the last place, he/she would like to go ever in life and why, the answer will have a scope of details.

Keep your tone friendly and polite: Conversations are not interviews. It is a social exercise and not a test on which you are to be evaluated. You do not need to worry about being confident or imposing. All you need is a friendly tone, genuine warmth, and politeness.

Most people keep worrying about being very confident or assertive when they talk to someone. It is not the approach required to begin a conversation with a stranger.

It would help if you remained polite at all times and reflected a genuine interest in the conversation.

Bringing Conversations to an End

Express your gratitude with complete sincerity: Everything has to come to an end at some point in time, and conversations are no exception to a rule. However, they must not come to an abrupt end.

It would be best if you learned to express your gratitude while ending conversations. Thank the person genuinely for the time and valuable insights and express what you gained from the conversation.

We can do very little for people around us, but even a few words of gratitude can help people feel pleasant, satisfied, and valuable.

You can also expect the same to come back to you, and that would help in boosting your confidence for future conversations.

CHAPTER 13: GETTING COMFORTABLE IN GROUPS

Introverts usually have a very tough time joining group conversations and actively participating in them. It is no secret, and there are some very obvious reasons for that.

What Makes Group Discussions So Challenging for an Introvert?

They are overwhelming: Let us be honest about this. Group conversations are very overwhelming for introverts. There are too many people and ideas get thrown left, right, and center. The thought that you'll have to speak in front of so many people can be dizzying. It is a prime reason most introverts try to avoid group conversations.

However, we all know that it can't be an excuse not to participate in group conversations. We all have to work in teams, and the free flow of ideas takes place in group conversations, and hence they are vital. You will have to leave your inhibitions and get habitual of them.

Don't allow enough time to think: When there are more people in the group, the flow of ideas is rapid. It can become a very difficult task for an introvert to process ideas at such a fast pace. While you are still pondering over the idea presented by one person, another one is thrown for discussion.

You might find it very tough to match that pace, and hence you will have to change your strategy. If you want to participate in the group conversations, you must stick to its central theme and present your idea if you have any. You can also pick the idea you agree to and then present your thoughts backing that idea. It will save you some thinking time.

It doesn't feel right: The major difference between an introvert and an extrovert is exposure. While extroverts are used to discussions in large groups and have lower inhibitions, it isn't the case with introverts. They feel uncomfortable in large groups are they are constantly trying to remain out of focus.

This tendency needs to be changed. In the beginning, the idea of talking in a large group may look repulsive, but it is the need of the hour, and evasions won't work in the long - run. Therefore, even if the idea may look challenging, you'll need to convince yourself to participate. You will have to come to terms with the situation and begin giving your inputs even if they are few and far between.

You do not get a chance to speak: It is an open secret that group discussions are primarily the playing field of extroverts. There are too many participants eager to present their views, and hence if you are thinking of speaking at your regular pace and intervals, your voice may remain unheard.

The only way you can get a chance to speak in group discussions is that you learn to interrupt others if you have some idea that is relevant at that place. Please do not feel ashamed to put your idea as soon as someone is about to put their idea. If you wait long enough, someone else might begin speaking, and you may not get the chance.

You may not be loud enough: Softly speaking is a good idea when you have a one to one discussion, and raising your pitch may not even be polite. However, that doesn't work well in group conversations as too many people are speaking at the same time and many more are eager to present their ideas.

Don't know with whom to make eye contact: Maintaining eye contact while speaking gives you confidence and also a conviction that your point is getting across to others. However, it can become a challenge when speaking in a group as there are many participants.

It is always better to have eye contact with the person you feel more confident talking to, and then once you have gained some confidence, you can keep shifting your eye contact to other members in the conversation. It will not only reflect your confidence, but it will also help you understand if others are paying attention.

Sometimes you may feel excluded: There will be times when you may feel excluded from the conversations. It happens when the conversations get carried away, and some people in the group take control of the conversation.

Even in that case, you can begin putting your point to the person sitting closest to you and present your ideas as a group. Such ideas will have greater force and support than individual ideas.

Tips to Get Better Share in Group Conversations

Use facial expressions to show your engagement: Group conversations have certain leaders, and others are adding to the conversations. As an introvert with low exposure, your engagement levels may be poor. You may also struggle with the points to put in the conversations. However, that shouldn't make you feel left alone.

Even if you are not getting to put too many points, you can be a part of the group by expressing your engagement through your facial expressions. Speakers, no matter how acclaimed they are, need the support of the listeners. If you are paying attention, you can even express your opinion through your facial expressions, and they will be recognized.

The spoken word is not always the best way to interact every time. If you are expressing yourself through your facial expressions, you can still become a contributing member of the conversation, and your opinion may be asked even by the leaders.

React to the things shared by others: It is yet another very important part to be remembered if you want to be treated as an integral part of conversations. It would be best if you expressed your reactions to things openly. It makes the speakers feel that you are paying attention to the conversation, and your opinion may be asked on the matter.

You must always remember that people love when others are paying attention to them. Even though speakers may not make it obvious, they are constantly looking for attention and approval. If you have been paying attention, and you can express that through your reactions, you will remain an important part of the conversation.

Calling people by their names would get their attention: The best way to catch the attention of the participants in the group is to call them by their names. Whenever you are presenting an idea or stating a fact, it is always better to identify the speaker to whom that might be directed and interact directly with that person using the name.

When you do that, you not only have the attention of that speaker but also have it from others. It demonstrates that you have been paying attention, and you may have specific points to put.

CHAPTER 14: LEARNING TO LISTEN

Listening is a key skill that is not on the list, especially of the extroverts. Extroverts are so pumped up to present their thoughts that they intentionally or unintentionally choose not to pay attention to what others have to say and remain focused on the points they want to put.

Even introverts or the people with poor social skills are not far behind in performing poorly in the listening department. They are so much engrossed in formulating their thoughts that they do not get a good chance to listen to what others are saying. They are living in their minds, and hence they miss the opportunity to listen to the core facts that could have allowed them to place their opinions better.

A big problem with listening is that most people do not know the core differences between hearing and listening.

Hearing is an involuntary action that can even happen by accident. You may be sitting somewhere or passing by and hear something. We mostly don't pay attention to such things. Hearing is an effortless activity. While you are getting things in your ear, your mind is not paying much attention to it. Here, attention is the keyword, and that can be a very crucial thing.

Listening, on the other hand, is a focused activity that you do voluntarily. It doesn't happen by accident, but it needs intent.

Focus not only on what is being told but also on what's being meant: You not only listen to the words being said but also pay attention to the message being conveyed. You'll need to focus your attention on the speakers and not just hear the words falling on your ears but also be attentive enough to read between the lines.

Ask relevant questions: Asking relevant questions is another important part of a conversation, and that can't happen until you have been paying attention to the listener. If you want to take the conversation forward, you'll have to listen to the things said by the speaker so that you can take the cue for your next question.

It is one thing that most people ignore and end up asking rhetorical or repetitive questions that may bring conversations to a premature end.

Don't pass quick judgments: We all like to believe that we have a unique eye to judge someone's character and intent; we largely forget that it isn't the truth. Making assumptions early on in a conversation can be termed as a sin. It is always better to allow people to present whatever they have to say completely. Do not pass quick judgments as that can make you lose your interest early on.

Sometimes repeat the things told by the speaker as you put forth your next question: Every individual saying anything would love to be reassured that the listeners have been paying attention. You always have a golden opportunity to express your attentiveness. You can repeat the main points stated by the speaker and then frame your next question based on those things. It helps on many levels.

First, it ingrains in the mind of the speaker that you have been paying attention to. Second, there are no notes to refer to in front of the speakers. They may be framing too many things in their minds, and repetition of some of the points also help the speakers in keeping their next answer precise. Most speakers appreciate it a lot, and you can get the potential to conduct a conversation meaningfully.

Show empathy: It is the most important part of listening properly. You must keep yourself in the shoes of the listener and try to understand the speaker's point. We all have an internal mechanism to begin discerning everything that crosses our ears quickly. It is a process opposing understanding. While you may be able to prove that you are smarter, you'll not be able to carry the conversation forward.

It is very important that you pay attention to things told by the speaker and also to the conditions behind them. You do not need to surrender to their idea, but you must reciprocate that you acknowledge and understand what they are thinking, feeling, or saying.

Active listening is a task that requires practice and patience. Most people do not want to invest both, and that's why they are never able to strike meaningful conversations or appear brash, garish, or even flashy.

Listening is an equally important skill as speaking if you want to hold meaningful conversations. However, both introverts and extroverts fail to pay attention to this necessary skill that they could master even with a little practice. Active listening can help you gain the attentiveness and sympathy of even the people opposing you in ideas.

If you want to become an active listener, you must bring the following things in practice:

Learn to drive yourself out of your thoughts: Introverts or people with poor social skills are always struggling with their thoughts as they are trying to come up with the next thing to say in reply. It is a self - defeating exercise. By the time you frame the reply of the previous argument, the speaker might have moved on to the next topic, and you might not even realize. It happens all too often, and people keep struggling with their inability to connect to others in conversations.

You'll have to understand that it isn't the chemistry that's missing but your attention. You must pay attention to the speakers and what they are saying, even if you are unable to come up with something very bright in reply. Your attention will keep you in the conversations.

It is not unusual for introverts to get lost in framing their thoughts, and hence you will have to drive yourself out of your thoughts and pay attention to the speaker. Never forget that you can always frame your next question taking the cues from the speaker's reply.

Learn to maintain eye contact: When someone is speaking, eye contact is the most reassuring thing to have. You'd expect the listeners to maintain eye contact so that you always remain assured that they are paying attention. It would be best if you extended the courtesy to all the speakers.

You must maintain eye contact with the speaker except when the speaker is trying to frame the points in mind. Eye contact is always a confidence - building measure.

Always show responsiveness: We all like it when people listen to us and keep responding intermittently. You might have seen that people on stage are always looking for applauses. Even hootings are not bad as long as they are expecting it because they get to know that they still have the attention of the audience.

It is the least you can do for the speaker, and you must not be hesitant in it. Always try to be as responsive as possible. It is always better to keep giving authentic feedback in the form of yes, yeah, I agree, so on and so forth. You do not need to be over the top or exaggerate your response, but the speaker deserves to know that he/she has been able to reach out to you.

If you do not agree with something said by the speaker, you can also bring that up politely at the end of the argument. Most speakers would feel flattered by the fact that you have been paying close attention to everything.

It can help you stand out in conversations, and you'd face no struggle in holding long and meaningful conversations.

Be genuine: Genuine concern and expressions always convey the meaning to the intended person, while artificial or exaggerated expressions always get spotted. You'll have to make a conscious decision whether you want to be a person to whom others can look up to or a person with too many artificial layers.

A good listener should be genuine in expressions and always careful of everyone's sensitivities. It would help if you showed empathy and remain concerned about the feelings of others.

CHAPTER 15: UNDERSTANDING THE UNSAID

Nonverbal communication holds an even more important spot than verbal communication as it helps you understand whether people are interested in talking to you or not, and also if they want to continue.

Many times, you rely on non - verbal communication for unsaid things, and it is not even possible to state every fact in black and white.

Extroverts can be bold and push their way into conversations. They may not fear a little ridicule or embarrassment. However, that's not the case with introverts or people with poor social skills, as even a little disapproval can break their confidence.

In such cases, understanding the unspoken non - verbal cues can help them initiate conversations and take them forward.

Understanding might seem to be a very generic verb, but it holds the secret power of lasting relationships. Most conversations, associations, and relationships prematurely end because there is a lack of understanding in them.

Taking cues from the non - verbal communication can help you in understanding the intent, feelings, and apprehensions of others better.

Initiating a conversation seems to be the toughest challenge for most introverts.

In this part, we'll discuss the ways to understand if someone is interested in talking to you or not.

Non - verbal Cues for Beginning a Conversation

Smile and wait for the reciprocal: Most people are never able to decide if someone is open to talking or not. Here, 'open' means okay talking to you; it doesn't mean eager.

Many times you may have eye contact with someone while you are just searching for someone to talk to. Most people will remain busy with their lives while someone might reply with a smile.

It is a cue that the person is open to conversation. It is a non - verbal representation of 'hello,' and you can move forward and rightly approach that person.

However, you would need to ensure that it was a casual smile and eye contact, and you hadn't been staring at that individual.

Understand the leaning sign: While talking in groups, you may not get equal attention from all the participants. Some will remain busy in their worlds as usual, but there will be a few who may show a keen interest in the things you may be saying. An easy way to identify such people is to see if they are leaning toward you. We tend to lean toward the people we agree to.

It is also a good way to find if someone is interested in talking to you in an alien setting. For instance, if you are sitting in a café, and you find someone leaning toward you, it might be the correct time to pass a smile and try to initiate a conversation. It is a signal that the individual might be interested in talking to you.

Elimination of physical barriers: When people are really hooked on to the things you are saying, it is an impulsive action to get things out of the way. You may find people removing objects kept in the way. These can be harmless objects that were not even obstructing the conversation. People can begin clearing things like cups, mugs, bags kept in the middle, and you can take a cue that the person is very interested in whatever you are telling. It is also a signal that the person isn't feeling alarmed from you.

Is someone looking in your direction?: We live in a strange world where most people are busy with their lives, and the ones that aren't busy are shy to approach others. You might have noticed it many times that people look in your general direction, but when you pay attention, they begin fiddling with something. Even you might have done that.

It is a sign that the individual is open to talk to you. You can look back in the direction of that person, and when your eyes meet, you can pass a smile. If you are not the point of attention, your smile may not get noticed. If it gets noticed and you get a smile back in revert, it could be a signal to begin a conversation.

Cues Signaling Interest in the Conversation

Contrary to what most people believe, engaging someone in a conversation is only one part. You must also understand whether that person wants to continue talking to you or not. If you do not take the cues, you might keep dragging a lifeless conversation too long. It can also affect your prospects of having a conversation again with that person in the future.

Do you see the effort: Good conversations need to have involvement. If you have to make all the push, then maybe this is not the right conversation to be in. It would help if you tried to see that the other person is trying to put some effort into taking the conversations forward. Are you being asked the followup questions? Is that person trying to know you better?

All these can be signals that the other person is interested in talking to you and looking for the grounds for conversation. You can also put your weight on taking the conversation ahead.

If you see the other person giving curt one - word replies, then it might not be the right time to engage.

Is there information sharing: It is another very important cue that you must pay attention to. If the person is trying to strike a conversation and take it forward, there will be mutual information sharing. If you have told something about yourself, even that person might tell something relevant to that. It demonstrates that the person is trying to lower the guard.

Sharing of information is a good signal that tells that another person is interested in talking to you and knowing more about you.

You must remain careful about not asking very specific or personal things and allow the information to be shared organically. Any push in that direction can make the other person feel unnecessarily alarmed.

The direction of the feet: We have discussed this point even in earlier chapters, and it is an excellent cue to know if a person is still invested in the conversation.

If the person is continuously shifting the weight from one side to another or has pointed feet away from you, it may mean that the person wants to take a leave now. It'd be better if you ended the conversation there.

The direction of the feet is a natural reaction. When someone is invested in a conversation, the feet automatically move toward the speaker.

That person may have some other engagement or might be feeling bored. Whatever may be the reason, it'd be better if you allowed that person to leave.

Physical mirroring: We tend to mirror the actions of the people we are interested in listening to. It is a very important sign signaling that the person is hooked on to the conversation. You may see the other person putting the hands in a similar manner or nodding in agreement. However, the people who want to get out of the conversation might express their indifference by retracting themselves from the conversation. They might sit with their arms crossed, and that can reflect that they might not be interested in continuing the conversation. If you want better clarity, you can also look at the direction of their feet.

Are the laughs effortless?: Effortless laughs are not indicative of something funny being told, but they express agreement to the conversation. If you are having a good conversation, you might see that person smile often and have effortless laughs often on various things.

In case the person is not enjoying the conversation anymore, you might notice that person fiddling with things and laughter would vanish.

Is there attentiveness?: Last but not least, you will have to observe if the person is still attentive to the things you are saying or there is zoning out visible. When people lose interest in the conversation, they tend to get busy with their thoughts.

If you feel that the person is not attentive enough, you can take notice of that and try to bring the conversation to an end.

Non - verbal cues are a very powerful medium that you can develop to understand if people are enjoying talking to you or not, and you can use this knowledge to improve your social skills.

You need to be aware not only of the words being spoken but also of the things that are not being said. It doesn't take a lot to understand these non - verbal cues, and they can help you in excelling in your day to day conversations.

SECTION IV
LEARNING TO SPEAK IN PUBLIC

CHAPTER 16: ANXIETIES ARE NATURAL - LEARN TO KEEP THEM UNDER CONTROL

Public speaking is a subject that can easily fill many people with dread. It is a fact that many people fear public speaking even more than death. They'd prefer to die than speak in public.

Most people wonder why public speaking is so hard while speaking is natural to us. We all can say things and even have opinions, yet when it comes to expressing those opinions in front of others, people begin to falter, stutter, feel anxious, and lose their voice.

The people who believe that people are afraid of public speaking due to their lack of knowledge or shy nature then I suppose you might be wrong. People, even with good knowledge and extroverted personalities, may find it hard to speak eloquently in front of large gatherings.

One of the biggest reasons for such fears associated with public speakings is the fear of exposure. We are always afraid that when we speak in front of others, our weaknesses might get exposed. We may come out as weak or anxious, which essentially we all are.

People are always afraid of emotional breakdowns. They fear that they might not be able to handle the pressure of so many prying eyes and may become weak.

Finally, there is the fear of scrutiny. When we have a one to one conversation, the risk of scrutiny is low. But when you speak in front of more people, the risk of scrutiny goes up as the familiarity goes down. You do not have the backing of identification with a person.

Therefore, any public speaking can make a person anxious. Introverts may begin to feel anxious even if they have to speak in front of a small group, while extroverts may feel the same level of anxiousness when talking in front of large groups. Nevertheless, anxiety and nervousness are common feelings when going to speak in public.

Mark Twain once said, 'There are two types of speakers. Those who get nervous and those who are liars.'

- If you begin to feel something moving in your gut or experience cramps, you do not need to worry because it is your mind feeling anxious about a lot of things.

Some of the physical symptoms of public speaking anxiety are:

- Shaking
- Blushing
- Shaky voice
- Breathlessness or shortness of breath
- Pounding of heart
- Dizziness
- Gut - wrenching feeling or even upset stomach

There is no way that you can fully eliminate anxiety. No matter how confident or prepared you are, there is something within that keeps you on edge, at least for the early few minutes, until you get comfortable with your audience.

While you are establishing contact with the audience, engaging with them, finding your flow, and relaxing your mind, there is some anxiety within you.

The more anxious people never pay attention to engagement with the audience because they remain tied up within their thoughts and are never able to recover during public speaking.

If you want to improve your social skills and become more confident while speaking in public, you will need to keep the following points in mind.

Tips to Lower Anxiety and Build Confidence

Learn to accept some anxiety: If you believe that there is a way to get complete control over your anxieties, you are living in wonderland. Have you ever seen gymnasts about to participate in the competitions? Those are the people with the highest level of training and knowledge that they are better than 99.99 percent watching them, yet you can see the anxiety on their faces.

Even the biggest stage performers in the world feel that chill within them for the first few minutes of their stage performance until they have owned the stage.

Most people falter on stage because they are never able to come to terms with their anxiety. As Mark

Twain had said, every person in the world has this anxiety. However, some people can fake confidence better than others.

Your anxiety is not your enemy. It is a defense mechanism to keep you alert. You do not have to work against it but address the issues leading to it.

Have the right perspective: Incorrect mindset is the biggest cause of anxiety in public speaking. Most people form a perception that they are being scrutinized rigorously, and hence they begin to fall apart. You must understand that you are not the center of attention of all the people around you. They may be busy with their thoughts, and you don't have to think about them, but the point you want to drive across.

The best way to do so if to keep your focus on the subject that you are discussing. Your perspective about that topic is important. Do not bother if people agree to it at that point or not.

There is no need to expect perfection: We all have a desire to be perfect in whatever we do. Especially when it comes to our public image, we do not want to have any blemish on it.

This approach can always prevent you from fearless public speaking. When you are speaking in public, there is no way to achieve perfection. People are entitled to their opinions, and hence those can always vary.

If you want to become good at public speaking, you will have to shun the expectation of being perfect.

Know the subject: There is no substitute for knowledge. Most people are so much worried about the people they are speaking to and their perception that they forget that they need to focus on the subject.

If you have command over the subject and you are confident about the facts you have, there is no reason for you to feel even a bit of underconfidence because, ultimately, knowledge makes all the difference in public speaking.

Engage your audience: A big reason people begin to feel underconfident in their discourses is that they are unable to engage their audience. It doesn't matter whether you are addressing a few people sitting across a table or a whole stadium packed with people; if you don't have their attention and engagement, it isn't going to succeed.

It would help if you involved the people around you in the discussion. It doesn't matter whether you need to maintain eye contact, invoke a response, or ask questions; audience engagement is vital.

Breathe deeply: Always remember that it is fine to be a bit nervous. You can't eliminate nervousness but have effective control over it through deep breathing. If you are feeling on edge, utilize deep breathing to calm your senses. It will help you quickly regain your thoughts and would also take away the stress on your face.

Stress can also make the muscles tense, and you may feel stiff. It can even deteriorate your energy levels rapidly. Deep breathing while you are talking, can help you in dealing with all these issues effortlessly.

Do not emphasize knowing everything: Knowledge is a tricky thing. There is no limit to the knowledge available. If you are nervous, you try to fill up as much knowledge as possible to compensate for the shortage of confidence.

It is a futile exercise. You do not need to know everything. It is better to know the things you know better than knowing a lot without command over them. Trying to know a lot also carries a risk of mixing things, and that is again a problem.

Maintain eye contact with the audience: The best way to remain confident and have control of your audience is to maintain eye contact. With a smaller group, it is easier to have eye contact with every individual. It may not be easy with a large group, but when you scan your audience with your eyes, it reflects your confidence, and you can connect with the audience better.

It would help if you always remembered that nervousness and anxiety are emotions that originate within you. There is no way you can get strength from outside. If you are looking for strength to counter anxiety and nervousness, you will again have to look within you.

If you want to be confident in public speaking, you can do the following:

Set specific goals for yourself: People do not have specific goals for their public speaking skills, and that's why they can never feel satisfied. If you want to do well in public speaking, you must have an objective.

It would help if you practiced with the target in view, and you'd find the overcoming your apprehensions would become much easier.

Practice at home: There is no alternative to practice. The more you practice, the more proficient you'll become. Hence, if you want to overcome your fears, you must practice pubic speaking at home. Practicing your pitch, tone, and dialect always helps. It gives you confidence as well as a feel of what the audience might get as a final product. This way, you can prevent unpleasant surprises.

CHAPTER 17: UNDERSTAND THE AUDIENCE YOU ARE ABOUT TO ADDRESS

When speaking in public or even in front of a small group, it becomes very important that the speaker gets a positive response from the audience or at least has a fair amount of audience engagement. Irrespective of how the audience is connected, the response is critical.

Connecting to a large audience can become tough for many people due to its diverse nature and the inability to have person to person connect.

If you want to establish a strong connect, you'll need to work on three different levels:

Know Your Audience

Knowing the audience is important as it helps you to deliver the right content. We all know that the things to which younger audiences can connect better may not work so well with the elder audience. If you try to come up with the same material with all kinds of audiences, you may not have the same kind of engagement.

Therefore, you must be well aware of the audience demographics. Things like their general age, gender, religion, educational level, culture, language, and affiliations are some of the things that would determine the kind of content that would work.

Even if you are there to make the audience laugh, one type of jokes may not work on all kinds of audiences.

Hence, as a speaker, you must be well - informed about the kind of people you are going to interact with. If you want to have a better audience engagement, your content must be prepared accordingly.

Analysis As You Speak

As you speak, it is important that you continuously analyze whether the audience is able to connect to you well. There are times when the audience feels a bit left out even when you are talking on the topic to be discussed. It can happen maybe because you are too technical or your talk is too simplistic, and the audience is not able to feel intellectually challenged.

As a speaker, you will have to analyze these things continuously until you find your flow. Once that happens, you will be able to drive your point across more comfortably.

Inciting Audience Engagement

When addressing a large gathering or even a small group, as a speaker, you get more time to speak, and the verbal participation of the audience is minimal. It can make some of the people in the audience lose interest, or they may get distracted by other things easily.

You'll need to realize that the human mind needs stimulus to remain alert. As a speaker, the onus of creating that stimulus is upon you. If you are not trying to get that stimulus by asking questions or taking feedback, the audience may not get involved.

Hence, if you want to excel in public speaking, you'll need to learn the art of keeping the audience engaged.

CHAPTER 18: GETTING HOLD OF THE MIND AND THE MATTER

Preparation for a public speech or presentation can easily take over your nerves. Let us be honest; it is never the lack of ideas but the excess of them that is at the root of the problem. We feel so pumped up and stressed that the ideas that had been spilling out of our brain dry out when it is really the time to deliver them in front of the intended audience.

Public speaking can be a nerve - wracking experience for most people, especially for those who do not do that professionally.

However, you can't deny the fact that these days public speaking of some sort has become a necessity. You need to present ideas in front of people in your job or business and even give presentations. It makes learning public speaking a necessity.

In this section, until now, we have understood the ways to overcome anxiety and ensure audience engagement. This chapter will help you in understanding the things you'd need to keep in mind to present the matter that can make an impact.

As I said earlier, it is not the lack of ideas that we suffer but the excess of them. We have so many things running in our heads before we get on to the real deal, but as soon as we enter the presentation scenario, everything dries up in the top - floor. Many people begin to look for ideas, although all the pointers are in front of them. It isn't the scarcity of material, but the pressure to perform that usually takes over.

If you want your public speeches or presentations to go smooth, you must ensure:

Do not let the pressure take over you: There should be no shame in admitting the fact that such public speeches and presentations can put a lot of pressure on people. They can have a deep impact on the mental, physical, and emotional health of the speaker too. If it is your first time or your previous attempts haven't gone well, the pressure can be insurmountable.

You are not the first and the last person to speak on the face of this earth, and this is definitely not going to be your last attempt at it, and hence there is nothing for you to take so much pressure. However, I'll not deny that I understand the kind of pressure it can build.

I only want you to understand that if you allow this pressure to take over your mind, it could get you into deep trouble when you are about to speak. This pressure will block your mind and also obstruct the free flow of ideas.

Although good sense would ask you to practice hard till the last moment, you'd get much better results if you stopped practicing a day before your presentation. Feel free before the presentation, and keep yourself distracted.

Most people believe that they might not be able to recall all the points if they do not revise, but they are wrong. They forget the value and importance of nervousness.

When you are nervous, which you will be when you are giving the presentation, your nervousness will lead to a strong adrenaline rush. It is an important hormone that numbs the pain sensitivities, makes you sharp, and helps you overcome forgetfulness.

Therefore, although you may fear forgetting things, nothing of that sort would happen.

There are no rules and standards for war: People would try to coach you that you must look confident, have such and such opening line, look in the eye, begin with a joke, do some storytelling, but none of that may work for you.

You must understand that every individual has a different coping mechanism, and you may work better with other settings. There is no way I can predict an opening line for you that'd work.

You'd need to find what works best for you. If you feel that you can begin well with a joke, go for it. If you feel that storytelling is your forte, you can begin with that as well. Some people can create a dramatic effect with numbers and statistics; if you are that individual, try it for effect.

There are no holds barred when it comes to such crucial things, and you are free to experiment with the style that suits you the best. The important thing is to find a style that can do justice to your personality. It would be best if you felt comfortable using that style.

Although presentations are about the numbers, a personal effect plays a very big role in how they appeal to the audience, and hence you must practice that well in advance. You can't be thinking about it on the day of your presentation or public speech.

You must know what you are talking about: Now we come to the heart of the matter, and that's the content. If you are giving a presentation or public speech, you must know that subject within its reaches inside out. There can be no alternative to this.

Your knowledge and expertise will give you the confidence that you'd require to give the presentation. You can't get that confidence from anything else. No amount of presentation skills, appearance, or the artful presentation of the slides can hide your lack of knowledge.

You must know the topic with great clarity because you will have to remain prepared not only to explain the concept but also to answer the questions that may be raised regarding that topic. You can be seen sifting through the files looking for the data.

Don't read your speech: This point is also a continuation of the previous point. You can't be looking for numbers and data points while you are giving your presentation. It is important to keep in mind that while you are explaining the points, you also have to ensure audience engagement.

When you are reading from a sheet, you will not be able to maintain eye contact, look for people having doubts, and ensure complete user engagement.

It can make your presentation boring and unattractive. There will be no charm, and you will be simply reading out a paper mechanically without any effect.

You have tools beyond words and PowerPoint slides: As a presenter or speaker, only the data with you is not what can make you appear effective and engaging. You also have multiple tools like your gestures, body language, tone, speed of delivery, pauses, and emphasis that you can use for effect.

Not every presenter is the same. You might remember some for their delivery while others have a very confident body language that can make you believe what they are saying. Even the tone used by the presenter and speed of delivery can have a powerful impact on the things being told.

How you appear matters: You will be the center of attraction, and hence many people will tell you to look immaculate and dress perfectly for the occasion to leave a lasting impression.

You must dress as per the occasion, but your focus should be on your comfort.

There is no doubt that the first few minutes of the presentation, how you appear, will matter. However, it would help if you didn't undermine the fact that for the rest of the presentation, all the focus would turn your voice and your eyes.

What you wear will become inconsequential, and hence how comfortable you feel within will matter a lot.

Therefore, dress as per the occasion but do not become obsessed about how you'd look and pay more attention to the way you are going to woo the audience.

Do not fret too much: In the end, I'd again like to reiterate that you shouldn't fret much about the whole deal and make it go over your head. Practicing is always helpful, but if you keep practicing it till the last moment, it can become an obstruction in itself because you are not going to perform a mechanical task. You are not going to do an assembly line task where following a process to the letter is important.

When you stand to speak, no process is going to help, and you'll be on your own. If you miss even one part of the overly rehearsed content, everything will get messed up.

Therefore, it is good to have command and clarity over your subject matter, but you shouldn't become obsessed with the process.

CHAPTER 19: IMPORTANCE OF CONTROL OF YOUR VOICE

Humankind, as a race, is obsessed with light and the ability to see. We lay so much emphasis on the capabilities of visual aid that we practically ignore the impact of sound.

Even the parameter of beauty for most people is the physical appeal. We love most of the things because they look good. Several flowers look enticing but have no fragrance, or there are other flowers with stronger and better fragrance.

However, these dynamics completely change when it comes to public speaking and presentations.

Although presentations are mostly audio - visual medium, yet do you think that people remember all those countless slides that you play during presentations.

It is one segment in which your voice matters. The power of pitch, flow, pauses, variety, and consistency are some of the factors that can have a deep impact on your presentations and public speeches.

Therefore, voice modulation is an important factor that you will need to focus on.

If you want to captivate the audience, effective voice modulation will play a very important role.

For asserting authority, you may need to raise your volume, but if you speak quietly, you can bring a calming effect.

Parts of Your Voice You Can Work On

Pitch: The frequency of sound can be high or low; it is called the pitch. Generally, women have a higher pitch in their speech, while men have a bit lower pitch. Recent studies show that if you keep the pitch of your voice a bit low, it gives your speech better authority.

Pace: Pace, as you know, is the speed. Most people speak very fast. It seems as if they have mugged up a lot, and they want to spit it out before they forget it. However, we all know that it isn't the case, and they talk fast out of habit. But, did you know it can give the listeners a hard time trying to understand what you are trying to say and also take away the advantage of adding some effect?

Studies have shown that speaking slow with defined pauses can have a better impression on the listeners. It doesn't mean that you'll begin speaking laboriously and bore the audience to death. I only mean to say that you should speak in a manner that everyone listening to you can understand you clearly without having to strain the ears.

Taking meaningful pauses before you are about to say something important also adds a dramatic effect to your speech, and the audience also gets to the edge of the seat to listen to you. It will also help you catch the attention of most of the listeners.

Stress: We all know that there are some words in every speech that will have a more dramatic effect on the audience. If you stress on those words, you can present them as keywords to alert the listeners to be prepared for something important or to relate to the topic deeply.

Variation: We all know that flat speeches are boring and may begin to make the listeners feel sleepy. The use of variation in the volume, pitch, tone, and pace can help you in keeping the listeners tied to your voice. Data shows that top TED talk speakers employ around 30 percent variety in their speeches to keep the audience glued.

Consistency: Another important thing to remember is that your facial expression and body language must match with your speech and its variations. It means that if you are trying to motivate the army to fight, you can't use a dull body language. The aggression you expect to raise in your men must be visible in your body language and facial expressions.

Ways to Improve Your Public Speaking Voice

Public speaking is a lot more about your confidence and the content you have for the listeners. However, it is an undeniable fact that effective voice modulation can give you much better reach to your audience, and the experience can be more immersive.

There is no doubt that some people are born with the gift of a powerful voice. It is the reason most of us are not singing chartbusters and remain happy listeners. However, that doesn't mean that if you do not have a very powerful voice, you are a pure disadvantageous position.

You can be a good speaker with any kind of voice if you have the confidence and content. However, working on your speech would definitely give you an upper edge and make you more engaging and accessible.

Learning voice modulation and improvement in speech quality doesn't take a lot of work, and you can do that even if you believe you do not have a very powerful voice.

If you want your message to get across to everyone, you can take the following steps:

Develop effective control over your pace: A big problem with most new speakers is that they want to get over with their speeches or presentations, and that's why they try to speak fast. It is also a kind of defense mechanism because when you are speaking very fast, your mind is not overthinking about stressful things, and hence you may feel less anxious.

However, there are several disadvantages of speaking very fast. First, all the listeners may not be able to grasp your point with complete clarity. Second, some listeners may feel irked because the whole exercise would require them to focus extra hard.

Third, you will not get the space to add the effects that come with stress and pauses.

Speaking at a slow and steady pace reflects your confidence, and you can employ all the voice modulation tools that you want.

Therefore, if you want to leave a lasting impression on the listeners and drive your point across, then you should speak in a loud and confident voice with a slow and steady pace.

Give your vocal cords some exercise: Even if you are born with one kind of a voice, it doesn't mean you can't change it. You must do vocal cord exercises to bring some strength in your voice. Reciting phrases or reading aloud will not only help you in building your voice, but it will also enable you to bring various voice modulations.

Record your voice and listen to it for better user experience: When you speak, you are not doing that for yourself. You speak to make others hear. In that sense, they are the customers. The better user experience should be your prime focus, and you can only do that when you can listen to the way you sound.

The idea may sound laughable, but it isn't. The way we hear our sound and what others listen, especially when it is passing through an electronic device, can be very different.

Record your voice and listen to it for voice quality, stresses, pauses, pace, and other voice modulations. In this way, you will get a chance to work on the weaker aspects.

Don't Undermine the Pauses: We have already discussed the importance of pauses. They add a startling effect to a speech, and you must learn to use them effectively. Taking too many and too long pauses can look bad, but when taken at the right place, they can make your speech captivating.

The full stops and commas in a sentence make it look effective, or else the whole paragraph would become a torture. You must try to explore this aspect and incorporate it into your speech.

Recording and listening to your voice can help you a lot in this direction.

CHAPTER 20: THE WAYS TO BE MORE CONVINCING

We all want to be convincing. There can be no two views about it. We all have a desire to be successful in our attempts, and the objective of public speaking is to convince or inform the listeners. However, we all know that most of the time, it is a tough task.

Convincing someone else about your idea will face resistance. It is natural. People aren't blank canvas sheets where you can easily write anything. They may already have something written over it, and you have the task to rewrite. It will be a tough task.

People are not going to take it from you if they aren't convinced that you know better. If they don't feel connected to you, they may not even pay attention to what you are saying; getting convinced is an entirely different story.

From your confidence, your style, to the way you put your ideas, everything will determine the impact. If you are not radiating positivity, it can also have a detrimental effect on your efforts.

In short, contrary to what most people believe, the power to persuade others is a skill that needs meticulous work. If you think that you have been failing at convincing others and that can be reflective of your personality, you need to rethink.

The art of persuasion doesn't come easy. You'd need to plan your talk carefully, tactfully, and meticulously if you want to get the desired results.

The list of things that can help you become more persuasive can be very long. Every situation may have its demands, and you will have to make suitable adjustments.

Some of the things that can help you in being more convincing are:

Knowledge - There is no substitute for it: When you are trying to convince others about something, you must understand that thing with great clarity. Most people think that they can deceive people with hefty terminologies and flaunt their knowledge. You are not there to flaunt your knowledge but to explain something to others the way you believe it is. If you think it is going to be an easy task, you are gravely mistaken to undermine the intelligence of the audience. People are not going to trust your idea until they are convinced that you know it better than them.

There can be no substitute for the knowledge, and hence you must prepare very well. You must know the concept better than anyone else in the room. You will need to prepare it in a way that you are capable of answering any doubt that arises in the mind fo the audience, or you think it is arising.

You must read more and then some more so that you are convinced of it first. You cannot ask others to believe in as idea even you don't think it works.

Connection with the audience: Establishing a connection with the audience is also very important if you want to convince them about something. The audience is not going to take it from you if it doesn't think that you have something in it for you, and that can't be accomplished without having a deep connection.

You must understand your audience and model your argument in such a way that the audience can relate to it. You must know the inclinations of your audience and the things that are going to be effective in that setting. You will have to understand their hopes and aspirations as they are the most porous points of entry.

Once you have the feel of the requirements of your audience, the battle is half one, as you will only need to probe it a bit, and then plant your idea as their need.

'What's there for me?' it is the guiding sentence with which everyone works. The audience is already convinced that when you are up there explaining something, there is something definitely there for you; it is now looking for something that'll make a difference in real life at any level. Until you can convince that there is something there for them, consider you are talking to a wall.

Your confidence is a power booster: You can't convince the audience about anything until it is confident that you believe in its presence yourself. Confidence is a very big requisite for convincing anything. You will never be able to drive anything into the minds of the audience until the audience can see the confidence oozing out of your personality.

You will need complete conviction about the idea and backing of knowledge to make others believe in anything. This confidence can't be superficial as such tactics don't work.

Shooting for commercials and telling a lie is something very different. There the actors aren't facing the audience, and they are simply reading from a script. When you are interacting with a live audience, such fake confidence measures won't work, and you'll remain frightened from within.

Making an idea click in the minds of others is a challenging task, and it needs much more than simple superficial arguments. Building confidence within is a task that you must undertake before anything else.

Learn to get down to their level: Big and complex terms may be good enough to prove that you know more and impress others, they can't be the correct tool to convince the audience about anything.

When you want your audience to understand something and get convinced by that idea, you will have to get down to their level and talk in a language and tone they understand. Hefty terms and statistics may be good enough for your opening statement, but if you want the audience to relate, you'll need to get down to conversational tone.

It is a style that takes some time to adapt, but it is the most effective way to make people feel what you are feeling or empathize with you.

Learn to tell stories: If you have every seen insurance agents selling you something very convincingly, you might have noticed that the stories they build are always related to you. Those stories have the power to make you contemplate seriously.

Stories have the power to make us think. Our minds are designed in such a manner that they are able to connect to our situations better, and stories can help very effectively in that.

If you want to learn the art of convincing others, you better learn the art of effective storytelling first and devise stories that are able to convey that point precisely.

It isn't that people don't understand the motives of the insurance agents and the story narrated by them. Still, they also understand the logic in the story, and most people can relate to it on a personal level. They know that the other person is only trying to make a sale but understand the thing hidden in it that can be beneficial for themselves.

Pay close attention to the structure and sequence of ideas: Proper structuring and sequencing of the ideas also play a very crucial role. If you begin randomly presenting your ideas, they will not have the intended effect.

It is always great to begin the conversation with a powerful introduction. You may want to throw in your relevant numbers and stats to catch the attention of the audience. You can use shock as an effect to make it more effective. The more shaken the audience feels, the easier it'd become to press on the next part.

Once you have created the effect, you must begin presenting your point. This part should be explained in detail. The audience must have a clear understanding of the concept. If the audience begins thinking that you are trying to hide anything or only putting one - sided facts, you may lose their interest.

Then you can begin explaining the reasons behind your beliefs and what are the tests they can stand.

You can even challenge the audience to think about it.

Coaxing, cajoling, and empathizing are some of the techniques you can use at this juncture because, by this point, the audience must consider you to be a part of them or a well - wisher.

Although, by this time, the audience may be considering your point, you are not home yet. There is enough space for doubts to emerge yet.

Your next step should be to give alternatives to the audience. They must get a chance to look at the other options they might have and ponder whether they can work better.

However, you are going to present rebuttals immediately to clear those doubts. Here, be thorough, and take your time. Do not rush or try to brush things under the carpet, or else you may appear to be defensive. It can give a big blow to your credibility.

Once there are no doubts, the turf is clear, and you will have convinced the audience about the importance of your idea.

You can conclude the argument on a positive note.

Involve the audience: The involvement of the audience at every step is important because you are dealing with real people. The moment you allow them to feel disconnected, you may lose them completely. Asking questions, looking for understanding, and clearing doubts are some of the strategies that can help you in keeping the audience involved.

Stay Positive: Positivity in your conduct is an important part of being convincing. If you are not positive in your attitude, you may lose the charm and appeal that is a very crucial requirement to make people think from your perspective.

SECTION V
OPENING UP TO THE WORLD

CHAPTER 21: INTERNALIZING THE CHANGE AND BECOMING SELF - AWARE

Until now, in this book, we have tried to understand the importance of social skills. Developing an understanding of the main reasons behind poor social skills gives you a chance to deal with them correctly. You know the reasons why you feel and behave differently than others and understand the main obstacles in your path.

A correct understanding of your weaknesses is the right way to overcome the challenges. Most people keep trying to incorporate social skill changes without understanding the specific challenges they face, and such cosmetic adjustments never work in their favor. They keep coming back to the square one and soon develop an inferiority complex and get trapped within the artificial cell of their understanding. This book has tried its best to help you prevent that from happening.

We have discussed various social skills in detail. From improvement techniques in conversation to public speaking skills, this book has given good weightage to both the segments.

However, to show any confidence and break the shackles of inferiority, you must realize your self - worth, improve your attitude, change your perspective about yourself, and brace yourself to face the world head - on.

Any work on your exterior persona cannot be very effective until you have really improved your inner persona.

This section will primarily focus on improving your inner self so that you can open up to the whole world in the true sense and not feel underconfident or insecure.

What is Self - Awareness?

In simple words, self - awareness is your ability to have the power of discernment to be able to understand your thoughts and feelings.

In our daily lives, we may feel several things, and these feelings can create a perception that those feelings truly represent us. That may not be the case most of the time. Our feelings can also be a result of specific incidents and situations. However, many people begin to treat those feelings as the true representative of their personality.

People begin to associate fear, shame, apprehension, and other such feelings to be a part of their true character. It can be very damaging to their personality. They may never feel equipped to make a sweeping change in their personality because their perception is incorrect.

Self - awareness can help you break this false perception of boundaries around you. It enables you to monitor the world within and outside you closely. If you are self - aware, you are less likely to feel deeply affected by every thought and feeling you may have. It can give you an objective way to look at things in life and not play by emotions alone.

Self - awareness is one of the basic requirements when it comes to bringing any real change in the personality.

Most people may think that when it is such an important concept, it should have been kept in the beginning. The placement of this segment at this juncture is not accidental.

When we were discussing the idea of presenting your speech convincingly, we discussed the importance of sequence.

We began the book with the causes of poor social skills and then focused on the prime area of fear and anxiety. These are easily relatable ideas. However, immediately after that, we began discussing the basic changes that could help you in improving your personality. From improving your conversation skills to developing public speaking skills, every topic is aspirational for every individual struggling with social skills.

However, now that you know the difference you can bring in your life with the help of this book, it is the right moment to internalize this change.

Most of us appear to be very strong and tough, yet we have a fragile inner self. Even a little criticism can make us coil back into the hard shell. We are unable to tolerate the fact that there may be a few things that the world might not like in us. However, we fail to notice that there are numerous other things that the world does like in us.

Weak discerning power if the proof of low self - awareness. In that case, we begin looking for validation from outside and rely solely on that. If you are in a position of power, it can encourage sycophancy. If you do not have considerable power or any significant position, it will result in underconfidence.

People keep on looking for measures to become more confident and likable, while they only need to be more aware.

Self - awareness is the practice of paying attention to your thoughts, feelings, and behaviors and analyzing their reasons. It helps you in making sense of the things occurring in your life.

Every new feeling, thought or emotion will not be able to take you down because you'd have a rationale behind it. You'd be able to make more sense of the world around you.

The best thing about self - awareness is that you can avoid having mood - swings. You become aware of your emotions, and hence you know the exact cause of every emotion you have. You don't take it as a sudden occurrence.

The best doesn't end here. We live in a world of quick - fix solutions, and they are the prime reason for most of our miseries. When we try to push minor problems under the carpet, we are giving them a safe room to develop and grow. Those problems never stay under the carpet for long. When they resurface again, they are stronger and mightier and need extra effort to be pushed.

Hurtful feelings, emotions, and bad moods, we all try to get rid of them as fast as possible.

- If you are feeling sad, watch a comedy
- If someone has hurt you, try to avoid facing that person again
- If you are feeling low, try to intoxicate yourself so that the mood is unable to affect you

These are avoidance techniques and not solutions.

You can feel sad due to a failure, a rejection, a loss, and several other reasons. Watching comedy will not change that reality. It is only going to aggravate the problem for you. When you are not self - aware, you try to avoid feeling sad and not work towards dealing with the issue so that you don't have to face it again. You get caught in an infinite loop.

Similarly, in case you have got hurt by someone or something. In place of looking at the amount of ego damage you are facing, you must evaluate the cause. People hurt you because you give them importance in your life. You allow them to cross certain boundaries where they begin to affect us. You can also feel hurt if someone has insulted you. In place of looking at the thing about which you have been insulted, you begin thinking about the ways you can take revenge or avoid that person forever.

These are not measures but mazes that don't take you anywhere. You keep running from one side to another, but ultimately you are going to get back at the same place.

Poor self - awareness will affect your communication skills, relationships, mood, decision - making process, productivity, and many such crucial areas.

Becoming self - aware is the stepping stone for social skill development. It would help if you did not forget that it is the fragile ego and poor self - confidence that keeps people locked in their shell forever.

If you haven't been trying to approach new people, that was because you were afraid of rejections. If you have not been speaking in your office meetings, your fear of ridicule may be the reason behind it. We always fear that certain things will be more hurtful, and that's why you consciously try to avoid them.

Self - awareness helps you in becoming confident, and you also get the power to analyze every such thought.

Tips to Improve Your Self - awareness

Stop ignoring your feelings: Most of us do not want to recognize bad and hurtful things in our lives. We don't want to be dishonest; we only want to postpone that pain. It begins a reactionary process with us. We become more focused on what we think. We stop paying attention to ourselves that may need improvement. It stalls the overall process of improvement.

It would be best if you stopped ignoring your feelings. Try to understand the basis of those feelings and take corrective steps about the causes and not the effects. Try to avoid the feelings is like shooting the messenger.

Self - improvement involves some risk, do not fear it: We can keep playing safe all our lives, but you must not forget that it is the desire to play safe that has kept you in your current state. If you want to change something about your personality, do not fear the world. Go ahead for it and take concrete steps like take a class, practice behavior alteration, read a book, or anything you may deem fit.

However, it would help if you keep reminding yourself that by merely thinking about it, nothing is going to happen. You will have to initiate an action. We keep worrying about the opinion of the world. Self - awareness is all about getting your focus away from the world and putting it on yourself.

Please pay attention to the things that bother you: The main reason we are never able to deal with some problems is not the severity of the problem but our absolute avoidance of it. As soon as that problem even crosses our minds, we try to shut everything down. You will have to learn to face the demons that haunt you the most. You can't survive as an ostrich that buries its head in the sand on spotting a hunter. You will have to remember that the hunter has spotted you and will enjoy the chance to have an easy meal.

If you stutter and you feel that it can make you embarrassed in front of others, you will have to face this fear. Do not avoid it. You can only get embarrassed once in front of anyone. Once they know, there is nothing new that they can know about it. However, the more you speak, the better you'll get at it. But, if you keep hiding behind an iron curtain of shame and embarrassment, you'll never be able to work either on your confidence or on your speech problems.

It is not your stuttering that leads to problems but your inability to handle it. The day you begin paying attention to the things that bother you and take a stand for them, they will stop bothering you in that manner forever.

Meditate: There is no better way to become self - aware than to meditate. When you close your eyes and focus on your thoughts, you become aware of their futility. Every thought that you have in your mind that has the power to bring you down originates in the mind. Most people live in the misconception that it is the impact of the external events that we have negative thoughts. There is nothing of that sort.

Bad events happen and then end. But you still have the thoughts. It is indicative that your mind is much more powerful than you think. Your mind produces the thoughts that can make you feel bad, powerless, underconfident, fearful, and embarrassed. These thoughts are a part of the larger protective mechanism. They are not needed.

When you meditate, you can focus on these thoughts and understand their futility as well as the use. Dealing with these thoughts or letting them pass away will become possible for you. There is no better exercise for the mind to become self - aware than to meditate.

It is easy and doesn't require much effort.

Meditation alone can help you in becoming highly self - aware, and you'll be able to identify whether a thought is really as bad as it seems and does it has the potential to do the amount of harm you think it can do.

We will practice a detailed meditation session in the next chapter.

Meditation at least once a day and preferably twice a day in the morning and evening can help you in feeling confident and aware. You will be able to relate to things better and manage your fears well.

Try to read people: While we are continuously over evaluating ourselves, we pay very little attention to the people around us. We fail to acknowledge the fact that even others have the same vulnerabilities and fallacies.

The more you try to read others, your understanding of the psyche of others would improve. You do not work in this society as a standalone unit. We all work as a team. When you are interacting with a person, even that person is interacting with you. Hence, only your action and reaction has no value until you also take into consideration the nature and reactions of others.

When you invest your time in others, you get to learn better ways to deal with different people and how the same action may invoke different reactions from others.

The more you'll try to read others, the more you'll become self - aware about your actions and reactions in those situations and whether they are apt. It will broaden the horizon of your understanding.

Identify the emotions that trigger you to recoil: Not everything is equally disastrous. While you are still trying to come out of your protective core, it is important to identify the things that may cause the highest amount of emotional response and the ones that you can to face bravely.

You should begin testing these emotions one at a time and not face sudden and united invasion.

Suppose you have stage fright. Try to look for the reasons for that stage fright. Was it embarrassment, or was there a comment that belittled you. Look for the right reason and begin working on the emotions related to it.

People are not afraid of the stage but specific incidents related to the event that may have a deep impact on their minds. You only need to understand yours and try to address it systematically.

Take feedback: We all have someone in whom we can confide fully. It can be your parents, your siblings, your best friend, or anyone else. No matter whom you choose for the task, but you must include that person in your awareness journey.

It would be best if you took feedback on the changes you have been making and also about the possible changes that you can bring. Such people are the strongest pillars of support, and hence you must find someone like that in your life. People have even confided in inanimate objects, but that doesn't matter much because there is nothing that you can't see if you wish, and you know all the solutions. The only requirement is of the will to implement those solutions, and you can do that with anyone or anything you deem fit.

CHAPTER 22: GUIDED MEDITATION PRACTICE FOR SELF - AWARENESS OF THOUGHTS

Sit in a peaceful place for meditation

Pay close attention to your surrounding

If there is anything is bothering you or distracting your thoughts, remove it

Get comfortable in your seat

Sit in a completely relaxed manner

You do not need to do anything

No action is needed at this point

Just sit completely relaxed for a few minutes

If anything important crosses your mind, jot it down in a notepad

Please do not make a mental note of it

You'd want your mind to be free of all kinds of thoughts

Deal with any thought running in your mind

Now, get into a comfortable position

Keep your back straight

Ensure that your shoulders are also straight

Your back and neck should be in a straight line

Place your hands on your thighs or lap with palms facing upwards

Now, close your eyes

Make slight adjustments by leaning forward and backward

It helps the body in relaxing completely in the position

Lean - to your left side and then to your right

Now, bring yourself to the center

Feel your head on your neck

Raise your chin a little

It will help you in placing your focus easily

Please try to feel your whole body

We are trying to become aware

You may know that there are all these things

But this meditation session is not about knowing

It is about becoming aware

We will try to feel many tangible and intangible things

Nothing in this exercise is futile

We do that all the time, even in real life

But, we are mostly doing it against ourselves

We keep making fears grow larger

We allow our confidence and courage to sink deeper

This meditation session will help you in reversing that

Please keep your eyes gently closed

Become conscious of your senses

Try to feel the sensations around you

Can you feel the air moving your clothes

Can you sense the clothes touching your skin

Do you feel any other sensation

Become fully aware of every sensation you can feel on your skin

Now try to listen to all the sounds you can hear

Pay deep attention

Can you hear the whirring of the fan

Or the sound coming from the airconditioning or the heating system

Can you hear any other sound in the background or the neighborhood
Any music playing in the back

Bring your awareness to smells around you
Can you smell the fragrance in the air
Does it smell fresh or stale
Does it carry any fragrance
Try to discern every fragrance

Now bring your focus on your body
Notice if there is tension anywhere
If you feel any part tense
Focus your complete awareness on that part
Hold it tight with your awareness
And then, release the tension
Adjust your body to release the pressure

We will begin breathing gently but deeply
There is no need to control your breathing yet
You do not need to worry about managing anything
Just keep your eyes gently closed

Breathe in
Breathe out

Breathe in
Breathe out

Breathe in
Breathe out

Do not let your awareness wander here and there
Just keep it focused on any one point
Look at a point between your eyebrows
It can be any point
Keep breathing

Breathe in
Breathe out

Breathe in
Breathe out

Breathe in
Breathe out

Before we more ahead
Ensure that your breathing has returned to normal
Feel the rhythmic pace
Feel the calm in your breath
The ease of the heart

Inhale
Exhale

Inhale
Exhale

Now we will practice deep breathing
Inhale all the air you can through your nostrils
Please do not do it with force
Keep inhaling at a slow but steady pace
Inhale as much air as you can
Fill the air to the brim
Keep inhaling until you feel you can't take in any more

Now hold it for a few moments
Let your body absorb this air
Allow the fresh air to penetrate the cell

It would replace the spent air

Then, exhale
Breathe out through your mouth
Don't be impatient
Don't try to push all of the air all at once
Just empty as much air as you can
At a slow and steady pace
Press your belly to the back to get all the air out
This process will help you in taking away all the negativity and stress

We'll again do deep breathing
Focus your awareness on your breathing
Do not think anything
Thoughts may divert your attention
Just acknowledge those thoughts
But do not engage with them
Bring your awareness back to your breathing

Begin inhaling through your nose
Feel the air coming into your nose
Keep your focus on your breathing
Try to feel its quality and characteristics

Now, hold the breath for a few moments
Allow the air to build some pressure inside you
There is no need to fear from this pressure
It will help in easing the negativity
When the pressure becomes unbearable

Release the breath through your mouth slowly
Do not try to expedite the process
It needs to be slow
It needs to be steady
Just keep your awareness tied to it
Observe the way calm is prevailing over your mind as you exhale
Push out as much air as you can before you begin inhaling again
Relax now
Breathe easy

Inhale
Exhale

Inhale
Exhale

Inhale

Exhale

Now focus your attention to your thoughts

Don't do anything

Simply become aware of your thoughts

Observe the thoughts coming to your mind

Don't take part in them

Don't be judgemental about them

Just observe the type of thoughts you are having

Remain indifferent from their nature

Such things don't matter at the moment

Just observe them objectively

It is normal to have negative thoughts

It shouldn't trouble you

These thoughts do not represent you

Just observe these thoughts

Become aware of your thoughts

Now, let us expand the awareness a bit more

Observe at a broader scale

Look outside your body

Think of the things that cause physical discomfort

Anything you can think of
Can you feel that pain now
Did you wince in pain thinking about it

There was no actual pain
Nothing touched you
You are fully awake
You are not sleeping
You are fully conscious and aware
Yet, you can feel that pain

The mind is much more powerful than we think
It can make us believe things
There is nothing to hurt you

Now, let us imagine
Think of a cloud floating above your head
It's a dark cloud
It's saturated
There can be precipitation
Can you get wet
It's not the time and place to get wet
Shift that cloud
It's not a tough job

You thought of the cloud
You made it up
You gave it the color
You can push it aside

Let us get back into your thoughts
There are many thoughts in your mind
All are not useful
It would be best if you become aware of them
Become objective
You don't need to struggle with your thoughts
They are only in your mind
They are not real
You can even push them aside
But, it is futile to fight them
Simply become aware of them
Learn to ignore them when needed
You don't need to pay attention to every thought

Think of people you know
Think of the things you don't like in them
Think of the things you like in them
Can you like them more?

Can you be more compassionate?
Can you become more tolerant?
Think of the things that agitate you
Can you help yourself better?
Can you control your mood?
Everything is inside you
You can control everything related to you
You only need to become aware

Now become aware of the things you feel when speaking to others
Think of your fears
Think of your worries
Think of the insult you might face
Think of the way others would mock
Now become aware that all that isn't real
You are making up all that in your mind
It was never real
There is no basis for this fear
No base for these thoughts
Become aware of the feelings

You are aware now
You know that you are in control
Your thoughts can't dictate you
Your mind can't run you
You are in complete command

Now bring your awareness to your thoughts
You don't have to participate
You are here to observe
Just look at the thoughts
They are not you
They don't reflect what you are
The thoughts in your mind are not a reflection of you

Simply observe your thought
Identify a thought that strikes you the most
Focus on it
Watch that thought closely
Do you identify it
Do you feel any emotion with this thought

Watch the form that thought takes
You don't need to change it

There needs to be no indulgence
Your participation is not required
Simply look at it

The mind has so many thoughts
They are not even connected
There is no reason to be concerned

Just maintain non - judgmental Observation
There is no reason to judge your thoughts
You don't need to bother about the kind of thoughts you have
No one is judging you
You also don't need to judge
You can simply pick and drop these thoughts
They are just like objects
There is no need for attachment
There is no need for resentment
Simply observe them
The form they take
The manner in which they come and go
Watch the speed of formation of thoughts
Observe the way they disappear

They aren't permanent

There is no reason to fear them

They are the creation of your mind

They have no physical form

You can make them disappear

Feel the power within you

Bring awareness back to your breathing

Watch the rhythm of your breathing

Is it stable

Are you breathing fast

Let it gain a natural pace

Now with your eyes closed

Focus your awareness outside

Try to feel your body

Feel the air on your skin

Does it feel warm or cold?

Try to move your toes

Do you feel it?

There can be a tingling sensation

Don't bother

It will go away

Breathe in

Breathe out

Breathe in

Breathe out

You are feeling calm now

You have a truce with your thoughts

They are not your enemies

But your thoughts do not rule you

Feel the calm in your heart

You are relaxed now

You can open your eyes when ready

Thank You!

CHAPTER 23: PREPARING TO FACE THE WORLD WITH CONFIDENCE

Facing the world with confidence is all it takes to break every old belief you might have formed about yourself. The day you decide to venture out with confidence, there will be nothing that would matter.

No obstacle looks big in such circumstances because your perspective would have changed. You would be looking at things objectively and not through the mirror of your past experiences or beliefs.

However, even getting out or stepping into the world as a different person can be a challenge. Things might be very different than what you may have been thinking of them. It may even take some time for others to change their perception about you. This whole exercise can become easy if you move one step at a time with some support in the beginning and then begin running on your own. Even soldiers need acclimatization of new terrains, and hence it shouldn't be a cause of shame for anyone.

Start with your old friends: If you want to get higher exposure to improve your social skills and have more confidence, nothing could be better than reconnecting with your old friends. Even introverts have friends, and in fact, they have closer ones.

If you want to increase your social exposure, your close friends can help you a lot. They can help you by introducing you to new groups and taking you to new places.

We can always talk freely with our friends as our inhibitions are low. You can practice your conversation skills with your friends. It would give exposure to practice various scenarios without the fear of feeling awkward.

Earlier, connecting to your old friends could have been such a difficult task. In the current age of the internet and easy social media connectivity, you can do that effortlessly.

Acknowledge and accept your flaws: We fear the most from exposing our vulnerabilities to the whole world as that can lay us bare. We fear that if the world gets to know about those things, you might become a laughing stock for others. It is the reason most people keep making desperate attempts to hide things from the eyes of others.

However, this can not be good for your social skills due to two reasons. First, the more you try to hide it, the less you'll get a chance to practice it. That part of your personality will never get exposure and hence might not see any development. If you want to make a sincere effort in developing that area, you must let the cat out of the bag in the open. Second, the harder you try to hide, the more ashamed and underconfident you will begin to feel about it.

Even if the flaw were not very big, a desperate attempt to keep it in hiding for very long would make you believe in its weakness, and even after several attempts, you may not be able to develop it.

Once you acknowledge that vulnerability, there would be nothing to prevent you from working on it in the open. You will feel more confident, and because you will feel more confident, you will have a better chance of developing it.

Be truthful: It is a golden rule that living with truth is much easier. Most people don't tell a lie because it is needed, but because it is convenient. They can avoid certain inconveniences temporarily, but it can't be a permanent solution.

Lies get exposed ultimately, and when they do, most people try to evasion. It can be the beginning of getting under the shell.

Telling the truth might look hard in the beginning, but it is a better solution as it opens you to the world to face it without fears.

You can face situations without having the fear in your subconscious that some of your lies can get exposed and humiliate you or even cause deeper troubles.

As you gain confidence, do not try to be selective: It is always better to have limited best friends and a good friendship with everyone. You may want to limit your exposure to your best friends in the beginning so that you can become more confident, but as you become more open, you must not remain selective. Try to expand your interaction as diversely as possible because that can give you the exposure you might have been looking for.

If you want to gain real confidence, you must talk to more and more people because then you'll get a chance to talk to people with different ideologies, mindsets, temperaments, and beliefs. It will keep challenging you constantly, and you'll get a chance to improve yourself continuously.

Get your act together: You can't become confident only by having good command over your speech. Confidence is reflective of an individual's character. If you want to reflect confidence from everything you do, then you must put your act together and do things that can help you in boosting your confidence.

Things like discipline, proper work ethics, and inner fire to improve are some of the things that can make you feel confident all the time.

If you want to bring changes that are reliable and effective, then bringing an overall change in your behavior is the best.

SECTION VI
STRENGTHENING FRIENDSHIPS
AND RELATIONSHIPS

CHAPTER 24: FRIENDSHIPS AND YOU

We all long for relationships, but this longing can be very deep in people with poor social skills or introverts. They keep feeling left out all their lives. It can easily turn into desperation. Many times, it can also fill the introverts with a feeling of inferiority and incompleteness. Loneliness and indifference can also crop up in such people.

Although friendships and relationships are important, they don't change you as a person.

It would help if you did not forget that lack of friends or loneliness is not indicative of all the factors in your life, and it definitely doesn't bring you to the end of the road.

Not allowing such things to take control of your mind or your emotions is very important.

You should keep in mind that:

Not having friends doesn't make you a bad person: When you are living a lonely life, it gives you a lot of time at hand that gets misused in overthinking. Most people easily jump to the conclusion that simply because they do not have too many friends, there might be something wrong with them. It is their mind that wants them to believe that because it doesn't like being challenged.

Having only a few friends doesn't make you a bad person at all. Many people may not have too many friends because they are too busy with their lives. They do not get the kind of time in their busy lives to think of saving time for friends. It is important to remember that friendships are time - consuming.

People may also not have too many friends as they like their older friends, and even after a change of place, they do not find the time and energy to invest in others.

Therefore, there can be several reasons for a person not to have many friends. The important thing is the reason that person doesn't have too many friends. You must not begin a blame game within you only for this reason.

You do not need to hide your loneliness or fake your social life: People with poor social life or no social life at all don't want others to know that they don't have an active social life. They keep feeling envious after looking at the active social life of others on social media platforms. They don't want to feel left out, and hence they are the first to boast about their personal lives.

However, this can even prove to be counterproductive even for you. When you boast about your large friend circle and your social life, people may feel apprehensive about joining you as they may fear that you are already occupied.

It can also put them under pressure, and in reality, you may not be able to cope up with the imaginary world you've been living in.

Honesty is always the best policy, and you don't need to feel ashamed of your laid back life with little activity, and you are more likely to find like - minded people soon.

It is perfectly normal to try to make new friends; it doesn't make you desperate or needy: Many extroverts are never able to understand the struggles of an introvert or a person who has been a victim of poor social skills. For them, not having too many friends may be an extraordinary event. Otherwise, for the rest of the world, having a few good friends is enough, and one doesn't need to have a very large circle.

Therefore, you must never come under the pressure of the thought that while others have a lot of friends, you have a very limited friend circle or don't have too many friends.

You can begin to expand your friend circle whenever you feel comfortable talking to people. Many people begin to fear that if they try to make new friends, they might appear as needy or desperate. First, no one in the world has got the time and interest to think so much about your friendships, and hence you can move ahead with your plans. Second, even if someone has the idle time to think about such things, that person doesn't know your life and its needs.

Having or not having friends is a personal choice, and no one in the world has a say in that.

You'd need to take the initiative: As a person setting out late, you would need to take the initiative for making the friendship. Most people are apprehensive about initiating a friendship as they keep thinking that it'd look odd. However, the fact is that you've started very late, and hence if you do not initiate, most people may not even understand your interest in becoming friends.

If you want to have a great social life, you'd need to venture out more often and try to meet as many new people as possible. You do not need to worry about the things the society might think as all that is irrelevant.

You may need to work hard to gel in: It is a fact that if you are thinking of finding new friends and you haven't had too many friends, you may feel that sometimes people show indifference. They may remain preoccupied within and have too many things on their head.

It is the true nature of society today as people are very busy with their lives.

There might be times when you may not get the kind of response you might have been expecting. Remember that the other individual might have something on the mind, and that could have resulted in such a response. You must not activate the sulking mode or begin thinking about the reasons for the same every time that happens with you.

Making friends is not a big deal: We are social animals. Making friend comes to us naturally. You may be finding it tough to establish proper contact with others or to have seamless communications due to some of the hurdles that you might have faced; for the rest of the world, it is as natural an activity as eating food.

You may be new to the whole process, and it may be taking time, but you must remain assured that you'll reach there.

Give it the time it needs: Although kids can make friends within minutes, adults may take much longer than that and may reject more people that they may be ready to be friends with. It happens because the kids do not have definite ideologies, a specific thought process, and affiliations. We like to be friends with only those individuals who are likeminded and eager.

With kids, this isn't the case at all. Anyone who has four limbs and the permission to play is good enough for them. It is the reason that making friends can take time for some individuals.

CHAPTER 25: MAKING FRIENDS AS AN INTROVERT

Making new friends can be a challenging task for an introvert or someone with relatively poor social skills. It becomes even more difficult when you have passed your school or college phase because at those levels, making friends is easier.

However, as you reach the working - age and enter the corporates or other work settings, you realize that the world is much more competitive than you could have thought and highly preoccupied with itself.

Earlier, the societies were a bit more tightly interlinked, and hence people had the time to talk to each other, and there were low chances of a complete conversation ban. However, even that has changed because most of the things have become electronic these days. People living in the same room do not feel the need to interact most of the time.

As an introvert, the chances of that happening with you are very high. Most introverts like to present themselves as if they don't need social contact. It is neither correct nor helpful. When you try to show that you don't need others, you close yourself for others.

People don't have the power to understand your heart; neither they have the time nor the interest. If you indicate a bit, the world around you would be quick to switch to another person more willing to reciprocate.

If you want to make friends, you will have to work on your people skills and become more open and receptive.

Some of the ways to help you make friends are:

Brush up your people skills: If you want to make new friends, you must learn to be more curious about others. You can't get something until you are looking for it. Try to know as many people as you can because that would increase your exposure, and you will have a better chance of meeting people who are also interested in being friends with you.

Another very important thing is to be warm. Always be as warm as you can with your friends because that would help in increasing the chances of finding friends and taking the relationships forward. Kindness, politeness, and a little courtesy can help you a lot in making others take you as a genuine person.

The third most important thing is to be open. Do not get stiff on meeting new people and have strong reservations. If you are trying to talk to someone, while you are asking things about that person, please keep revealing relevant information in bits and pieces, even about yourself. People see it as a genuine attempt to begin a friendship or at least a conversation that can go ahead.

Please don't be nervous: We all feel nervous when meeting new people because there is a lot of unpredictability. There are too many variables for you to be certain. However, if you remain nervous for too long, you might even signal the other person to feel alarmed.

The best way to approach others is to be meet without preparing a lot. Do not worry about the best opening lines or something. While talking too, as long as you are not rude or offensive, you can say anything keeping mind the sensitivities of the other person. You'd only need to be a little emphatic and not very intelligent for this.

If you are concerned about any part of your behavior to be very odd, try to visualize if someone else has that same would you have bothered much. Most of the time, we are just overthinking about such things and yet doing nothing about improving them.

At times, your mind can get too much focused on how others are doing; you must put all your focus on your conversation. Do not bother about others and try to live in that moment.

Frequent some places: If you want to make new friends, you should try vising the same places again and again. It increases your familiarity not only with the place but also with the faces and the kind of people frequent that place. Your chances of making new friends would increase many times because even other people there will be noticing you.

It helps in lowering the inhibition levels, and even with a little effort, you can begin a conversation with others.

These days there are several sites and mobile apps that can help you make friends; however, introverts may use them cautiously.

When you are meeting too many people too regularly, your understanding of people gets better than introverts. You are also better suited to handle tough situations like avoidance, rejections, and cheatings.

The world of online friendships is very treacherous. As an introvert, you may find it difficult to navigate. Beginning the conversations is always easy because there is no fear of face to face rejections, and you know for sure that the other person is also looking for friends. However, you may face difficulties in taking it forward.

Volunteer: Another good place to make new friends is through working as a volunteer. While we may be working with a very large number of people at our workplace, making good friends becomes very tough there due to the competitive angle involved. However, when you meet someone while volunteering, there is no such competition involved, and hence people can have a pretty laid back attitude.

Take the initiative and show intent: When you are meeting new people, it is important to show that you intend to become friends. Most people are waiting for others to take the initiative. Even in that, you may make friends, but your rate of friendships would be almost half. Do not be hesitant about showing your intent to be friends with others.

When you talk to others, try to take the conversations forward and be encouraging. Ask questions and followups to make the other person feel that you are interested to know more. Keep giving information about you so that the other person also gets to know about you.

Plan for future meetups so that this friendship can be taken forward, and it doesn't become another one - off incident.

Be open to mistakes: In the end, friendships are not transactions or business deals. There are times when we all become relaxed and make mistakes. It can happen from your side or the other side. You will have to learn to be forgiving and accepting in nature.

CHAPTER 26: SECRETS FOR INTROVERTS TO MAINTAIN HEALTHY RELATIONSHIPS

You can easily be friends with an individual having a personality that's poles apart, and yet you may not find it that difficult to manage.

However, you may find it excruciatingly painful to bear even minor differences when you are in a relationship with someone. Most people find the reasons tough to explain, but it isn't that difficult.

In friendships, the relationships are based more on giving. Also, there are very compulsions, and hence people find it easy to manage.

The relationships, on the other hand, are based on sharing. Both partners expect many things from each other, and hence it can lead to friction, a feeling of unfulfillment, and dissatisfaction.

Relationships can be very delicate as they keep on taking the burden of all the past mistakes, and hence it can be difficult to know which blow might become the final blow.

While it is always a tight rope walk for people to maintain a healthy relationship, it can be even tougher for an introvert or a person with poor social skills.

Relationships can be demanding in nature, and you may have to relent for many things that you'd not normally do. Introverts may not show any resistance in making adjustments and compromises, yet there can be situations that may become unbearable for them.

In this chapter, we'll try to understand the various situations that can put introverts into a quandary and the ways that can help them manage the situations better.

Conflicts are natural, but how to deal with them: You must remember that as a rule of thumb, more than 60 percent of all relationship conflicts remain unresolved. Yet, those relationships last longer than one of the partners. Healthy relationships are not without conflicts. The secret of a happy and healthy relationship doesn't lie in the absence of conflicts. It depends on your ability to deal with those conflicts and manage them successfully.

People with poor social skills tend to avoid problems and brush them under the carpet while your partner may keep bringing it up on and off. It can quickly escalate and lead to chronic tensions. While having to face that problem on and off may look disturbing to you, the real problem lies in your manner of dealing with the issue.

You must understand that pushing the problems on the back burner doesn't solve them. You'll need to learn to address them as and when they arise. When you begin showing interest in addressing the problem, it will also help your partner in understanding the problems you may be facing. It is a two - way street.

Building a communication bridge: Effective communication is a key requirement for any healthy relationship, and that's an area in which you may face the biggest challenge. While for your partner, talking may be the key means to solve most of the problems, you may keep running away from it.

Some people get recharged when they discuss their problems and find a solution for them even when they are just discussing them. It can be the opposite for you who may have a hard time thinking rationally while you are struggling to form the best thing to say at that moment. It can be a real challenge in a relationship as it can break the communication bridge.

No matter whether you are an introvert or an extrovert, communication is the key to any relationship. In such circumstances, you must discuss this communication need with your partner at the beginning of the relationship.

While introverts and extroverts are poles apart in their nature, it is also a proven fact that opposites attract. Many extroverts love the company of their introvert partners because the relationship is symbiotic. Extroverts love to talk, and introverts have no problem listening. Partners can devise several ways to communicate even in non - verbal ways and maintain the relationship only if they are committed to taking it ahead.

Catering to the needs of your partner: Developing an understanding of the partner is a must for a healthy relationship. Most people discuss their needs, and hence they can communicate. Introverts have some limitations in this regard, and hence they will have to rely on verbal cues for holding the relationship stronger. Lack of verbal communication cannot be used as an excuse for not understanding the needs of your partner.

Dealing with the tempting idea of fixing your partner: This is a dangerous idea that can crop up in the minds of any partner. In some cases, it can arise in the minds of both the partners at the same time. There can be no worse idea than trying to change your partner for better or for worse.

There is no way you can execute that plan without having to feel disappointed in the end and also make your relationship suffer. People are not objects, and they don't change, at least not by force or compulsion. There is a high probability that your partner may agree to whatever you are saying. On a gunpoint, people even accept murders they haven't committed. The partner may even have decided internally to follow it to the letter. However, there will be moments when the partner would think of taking one chance, and then the same thing would begin.

It is a futile attempt in its entirety, and it must never be attempted at all. The only person in whom you can bring any change is you. You can sit and find out midway and expect your partner to falter at times and also remain prepared to forgive your partner when that happens genuinely.

Relationships can only work on working with each other and not by trying to change your partner.

Different personalities, different goals: You may be a completely different personality than your partner, and this means both of you can have different goals. The places where your partner may feel liberated may look like incarceration to you. It is nothing strange or new. Not only in the case of introverts, but almost half of the world's married couples may be struggling with it.

Both partners must understand the different goals of their partners and give them the respect due. There should be no encroachment or invasion of personal boundaries.

Finding ways for togetherness: Spending time together can have several meanings. Countless couples may be physically close but may have no connection on the intellectual level. Some couples may find it easy to connect but not enough inspiration or motivation to do so. Yet, such relationships keep on dragging for years. They can be mended easily, but no one takes the initiative to do so. You must understand the need for togetherness, and although both the partners may have different goals, you should find time to enjoy the company of your partner.

CONCLUSION

Thank you for making it through to the end of this book; let's hope it was informative and able to provide you with all of the tools you need to achieve your goals, whatever they may be.

Social skills are as important as our general communication skills, yet the amount of attention they get is minimal. People believe that only the ones walking the corridors of power need to learn social skills as they need to address large gatherings and convince the multitudes. It is a misconception that needs to be changed.

We live in a society. We can't survive without it. Humankind has been living in groups since time immemorial. It is time people pay attention to the basic skills that can make your conduct more convincing and effortless.

Learning proper social skills, even for ordinary people, is a challenging task due to the lack of awareness in society. It becomes an even more difficult task for introverts and people with poor social skills.

The society takes it for granted that every individual will have similar social skills, and hence there should be no problem in communication. However, we all know it better that not everyone is the same when it comes to social skills. Introverts have a very hard time surviving in a word where people don't cease talking.

The objective of this book has been to explain the concept of social skills and well as its tool for introverts and people with poor social skills.

This book has tried to explain all the major tools and concepts so that public speaking, as well as the casual conversation, doesn't remain a challenge for you.

Through this book, I have tried to explain major parts of social skills in detail so that you face no difficulty in applying them in your life.

This book would help you understand various ways to enhance your social skills.

It would give you a detailed account of all conversation and public speaking strategies and also ways to open up to the world with confidence.

I hope that you will be able to gain full advantage of the information provided by this book.

Finally, if you enjoyed this book, please let me know your thoughts with a short review on Amazon. It means a lot, thank you!

www.ingramcontent.com/pod-product-compliance
Lightning Source LLC
Chambersburg PA
CBHW070100120526
44589CB00033B/734